A

Fools' Names,
Fools' Faces

Fools' Names, Fools' Faces

Andrew Ferguson

With an Introduction by
P. J. O'Rourke

The Atlantic Monthly Press
New York

Published simultaneously in Canada
Printed in the United States of America

FIRST EDITION

Library of Congress Cataloging-in-Publication Data

Ferguson, Andrew, 1956–
    Fools' names, fools' faces / Andrew Ferguson; with an
    introduction by P. J. O'Rourke. — 1st ed.
        p.   cm.
    ISBN 0-87113-651-1
    1. Popular culture—United States.   2. Fads—United States.
    3. United States—Social life and customs—1971–   I. Title.
    E169.04.F465   1996
    306.4'0973—dc20   96-16377

Design by Laura Hammond Hough

Atlantic Monthly Press
841 Broadway
New York, NY 10003

10 9 8 7 6 5 4 3 2 1

Fools' names, like fools' faces,
Are often seen in public places.

Contents

Tom Foolery

Acknowledgments

"Nixon's Nemeses," "A *People* Person," "Saying It with Flowers," "From the Mouth of Babs," "The Soft-Rock President," "Bob McNamara's Brand," "Bad Girls Don't Cry," "A Sea of Stars," "The Look That Killed a Congressman," "A Very Unimportant Person," and "A Coffee Thing" originally appeared in *National Review*, as installments of "The Gimlet Eye" column. I wrote the column for four years, off and on —an inexplicable indulgence on the part of the magazine's otherwise sure-footed editor, John O'Sullivan, and his able lieutenants, Geoffrey Morris, Matt Carolan, and Linda Bridges. During those years my column alternated with Florence King's on the back page of the magazine; following Florence King is a nearly impossible task that I would not wish on any writer. The one compensation was that Florence became a trusted friend, convincing me that she's not the horrible misanthrope she claims to be. She's the sweetest misanthrope you can imagine.

"Next Question, Please," "Hit 'Em Again!" and "Final Copy" originally appeared in *Forbes MediaCritic*, where Terry Eastland allowed me to write about several of my many embarrassing adventures in journalism. Terry's intelligent editing ensured that I didn't embarrass myself more than I had to.

Jack Limpert made the risky decision in 1993 to hire me as a senior writer at *Washingtonian* magazine, where "My Night with Gennifer," "I've Got Virtue," "Trust Us: The Mystery of the Supreme Court," "Newt Gingrich's Opening Day," "Chasing Rainbows," "Alice in Cyberland," "I'm Terrific, You're Terrific," and "Dumbing Down" originally appeared. Jack's flyer was all the riskier because I had been out of journalism for a year, writing political speeches, and I was unsure whether I could write anything that didn't sound like watered-down Churchill. Jack's careful hand, along with the sympathetic guidance of Ken DeCell, wrung all the bad habits out of me, or a lot of them anyway. Unfortunately, now all my political speeches sound like watered-down Liebling.

"Low Profiles," "Sinatra at Eighty," "Don Imus's Sacrilege," and "Gorbachev and the Global Brain Trust" originally appeared in the *Weekly Standard*, where I am a senior editor. I owe thanks and much else to my bosses there, John Podhoretz, Bill Kristol, and Fred Barnes, and also to my friends and colleagues Chris Caldwell, Claudia Winkler, Richard Starr, Jay Nordlinger, and the two Davids, Brooks and Tell.

"The Donald Writes a Book," which originally appeared in the *Wall Street Journal*, was commissioned by the *Journal*'s then books editor, Manuela Hoelterhoff. That job was the least of the countless favors Manuela has done me—more than I can ever repay, and she is nice enough not to ask me to try. My thanks also to the *Journal*'s Bob Bartley.

"Bill Moyers and the Power of Myth" originally appeared in the *New Republic;* my thanks to Andrew Sullivan, who had the nerve to commission the piece and the guts to stand fast when the fur flew.

"Choice Cuts," "Puff the Magic Dragon Goes to Jail," and "Jesse Jackson's Old Pals" originally appeared in the *American Spectator*, and so, as a matter of fact, did I. Twelve years ago I was a graduate student in journalism at Indiana University, enjoying a dreamy second childhood and thinking that maybe someday I might just go out and get me a job. Then Bob Tyrrell, the magazine's editor-in-chief-for-life, offered me one. Actually, from that day to this, he has offered me much more than that. Bob, Wlady Pleszczynski, and Ron Burr quickly became my advisors, editors, barmates, and three of the truest friends I've ever had. This book wouldn't exist without them.

And it wouldn't exist without P. J. O'Rourke. His introduction is only the latest and most visible kindness of the hundreds he has done me over the years. For one thing, he introduced me to his gifted editor and friend, Morgan Entrekin, who is now my gifted editor and friend. Several other editorial hands have passed over some or all of these pieces. I've benefited especially from the wisdom of Jack Shafer, Ed McFadden, Nick and Mary Eberstadt, Paul Lindblad, and Joanne Innes, and my brothers Rick and Stan. It goes without saying that any mistakes in this volume should have been caught by them.

Finally, nothing in my life—and I mean nothing—would be possible without my wife, Denise.

This book is dedicated to her, to my father, and to the memory of my mother.

Introduction

ANDY FERGUSON WRITES ABOUT THE TERRIBLE
division in American society—the division between those who
believe in reason, God, and liberty and those who believe that
David Gergen went to work for the Clinton administration in
order to be true to himself. It may be an unbridgeable gap.
There's us, the people who hold a certain few truths to be evi-
dent. And there's them, the people—David Gergen, Bill Moyers,
Barbra Streisand, Louis Farrakhan, Mikhail Gorbachev, Bill
Clinton, Bill Clinton, Bill Clinton—who are willing to believe
anything. *Anything.* Anything at all. Anything on earth. Anything you can imagine and plenty of things you can't. That is,
they're willing to believe anything as long as that belief reflects
well on them. The characters in this book swell like weenies
on a grill, near to splitting their skins with pride over their belief
in diversity, social justice, compassion, sensitivity, fairness,
world peace, New Age enlightenment, and—first, last, and
always—themselves.

So this is really a book about self, though not about Andy
Ferguson's self, more's the pity. What a kind, generous, de-
cent volume that would be. But the reader will have to wait
and be satisfied with a cruelly funny book in the meantime.
Fools' Names is about the self-regarding self, about the self
of self-sanctimony, self-satisfaction, self-approval, self-love,

and self-realization, the self besotted with self-esteem, the taking oneself seriously self, and, of course, about all those selfless selves helping us help ourselves with self-help.

There's nothing surprising about the modern cult of the self. The I has been forever interested in the me. Humans naturally possess feelings of tenderness toward their own tender feelings. Until recently, however, most people were too busy working, raising children, dying young, and so forth to have time for full-blown conceit. Nor did religions or philosophies encourage *vanitas*. But philosophy has been repaired in this matter, theology too, and there's plenty of leisure in modern life.

> *Pickle your brains in a bottle,*
> *Put your heart up on the shelf,*
> *It's time to go a-fishing*
> *In the sewer of the self.*

Some of the fools described herein are merely egotists. Frank Sinatra, Donald Trump, and Robert McNamara have made careers of selfishness, and Gennifer Flowers has tried to. But most of Andy's mooncalf narcissists are confessed (and convicted) do-gooders. And these pious humanitarians are all collectivists of one kind or another, advocates for the expansion of political control over the lives of individuals. How did pinkos wind up immersed in the huggy-thought of the Me Decade (or, as it has become, the Me Eon)? What happened to the masses? Where did dialectical materialism go? Is my inner child going to be much use manning the barricades of class warfare?

Actually, yes. Self-seeking is valuable to the Left. There has always been an element of infantile greed to left-wing programs. The ideal behind property-in-common is a promise of something for nothing. And the reason you have nothing now, say those who preach this ideal, is that somebody took it. The vast wealth of the ——s (fill in the blank: Rockefellers, Jews, multinational corporations, members of the Trilateral Commission, whatever) is rightfully yours. And here lies the difference between "self-esteem," which Andy Ferguson finds everywhere touted, and "self-respect," which is never mentioned by anyone nowadays. Given the opportunity to steal one hundred dollars, someone with self-respect says, "I'm not the kind of person who would do that," while someone with self-esteem says, "I'm important! I'm worthy! I'm doing this for myself! Gimme that one hundred dollars!"

Also, all the other enticements of collectivisim have disappeared. Socialists promised economic efficiency, human equality, and personal liberation. This became an ugly jest everywhere socialism was tried. But the do-gooders can still vow to let you be a pig.

Given the horrible proofs of the twentieth century, it should be impossible to believe in collectivism or crackpot idealism of any type. But here, also, the self comes to the rescue. If, when theorizing, I look only inward, if I eschew all empirical evidence, if I ignore the entire outside world, then I'm free to create any fantastic scheme of ideology I like. It's not important what effects this ideology would have if it were put into practice. It's not important whether this ideology works. What's important is that *I* think it's right. *I* think it's fair. We have come to a point in ethical thinking where the idealists tell us that, as Andy puts it, "self-absorption is altruistic."

Thus Andy Ferguson has created a sort of unified field theory of all modern life—a single formula that in one broad sweep manages to explain the Clinton administration, the Lollapalooza rock tour, and Ricki Lake.

But Andy is no trifling social commentator satisfied with pontificating on contemporary evils. He is also an angry and exasperated man, an *homme engagé*, an activist who would

like to take the people indicted in this book, grab them by their
. . . And here we have a problem. Andy Ferguson is a nice guy,
a kind and charitable person, a Christian in both form and
content. . . . grab them by their consciences, perhaps. Though
it is just possible that Andy, if really provoked, might be convinced that the fools should have their mouths washed out
with soap—soap manufactured by a multinational corporation, a corporation with glass ceilings, that donated money
to GOPAC, had a spotty environmental record, and *did* test
its soap on animals. However, there are obstacles of legality
and logistics to such a plan. Andy must use weapons other
than Dial and Tide.

Beliefs that are stupid, dangerous, and sometimes insane
come forth in their legions from the American Society of
Newspaper Editors, the Hollywood Women's Political Committee, the Supreme Court, the State of the World Forum, the
Internet, the National Multicultural Institute, and your local
school system. Against these Andy arrays logic, common
sense, knowledge of history, principles of freedom, respect
for tradition, and—the one thing to which solemn folly has
no response—jokes. (Well, solemn folly does have Al Franken.
But, what with being an alum of post-1980 *Saturday Night
Live*, starring in *Stewart Saves His Family*, and serving as butt
boy to the Clintons, Franken is very busy walking the line
between telling jokes and being one.)

Andy wins. The fools are capped and belled. They are
dressed in the motley of their ridiculous opinions and set down
to a mock feast and made to eat their words. Gales of sen-
sible, majoritarian laughter greet the self-appointed preten-
sions, the self-important posturings, the self-absorbed prattle
as the fools hold court. Andy has given every ass in America
its ears and its tail. Can the knaves and villains pilloried in
this work ever bear to look themselves in the face again?

Alas, yes. There's a large mirror in the green room at every
TV studio. Those ears are going to need makeup—and some

styling gel on the tail, too. Because you can bet the fools will be on the Sunday morning public affairs shows. Probably with David Gergen.

P. J. O'Rourke
Washington, D C.

Court
Jester

Hit 'Em Again!

September 1994

AS A JOURNALISTIC HIT MAN, I AM DEFINITELY second or even third tier, ranking far below such masters of our craft as Sally Quinn, Stephanie Mansfield, R. Emmett Tyrrell, or Christopher Hitchens. But I will say this in my defense: I once called David Gergen a "goggle-eyed melon head."

This was in 1986 or 1987, in *Washington City Paper*. The phrase came offhandedly as I was in the midst of composing a thoroughly unprovoked hit on the real estate mogul and publisher Mort Zuckerman, Gergen's boss at *U.S. News & World Report*. I'd never heard of Zuckerman before the assignment, but even then his magazine column was taking on the aura of legend, and an editor friend told me that if I read several in a row I would feel compelled to insult him in print. How right my friend was. My piece was astoundingly salivary. I said—and my quotes, I think, proved—that Zuckerman's column was the worst in the history of opinion writing. (It has since got worse, by the way.) As the bile flowed, I started sputtering in all directions, and when, in a discussion of Zuckerman's truculent management style, it came time to mention Gergen, the insult appeared unbidden. My editor, a man as heedless as I, let it stay.

The piece was published a few weeks later and made some noise, especially in the offices of *U.S. News*. I didn't give the

Gergen insult a second thought—it came, after all, amid a torrent of similarly tasteless abuse directed at Zuckerman, a far larger target—until a friend at *U.S. News* told me that some prankster had snuck into Gergen's office one evening and placed a melon on his desk. I tried to laugh but in truth felt uneasy. Had I gone too far? About six months later, I was inadvertently introduced to Gergen at a party. He didn't recognize my name, but soon a little light bulb went on. His eyes—I'm sorry, there's no other way to put it—popped out like a pair of goggles. He said, "Oh, God," and turned away. *Oh, God* is right. I felt terrible. Should I write him a note? Send flowers or a box of candy? (A fruit bowl was out of the question; they might throw in a melon.) I never did any of that, needless to say. I just went through the next several years feeling like a heel.

You don't feel sorry for me, of course, and you're not supposed to, for my little anecdote has a happy ending. One fine spring day in 1993 all my self-recriminations vanished. I turned on the television and saw Gergen standing in the Rose Garden at the White House with his new boss, Bill Clinton. The one-time salesman of Reaganism enlisting in the cause of undoing Reaganism! It was a move of such staggering cynicism that the next day, when I overheard a colleague disparaging Gergen, I proudly butted in: "I called him a 'goggle-eyed melon head'!"

"If you're afraid of going too far," says Michael Kinsley, "you won't go far enough." This is the boldly obnoxious motto of the journalistic hit man, the guy or gal who earns a reputation for writing nasty things about people who are widely esteemed. Actually I do think I went too far in calling attention to Gergen's physical anomalies—his Ike-like glabrousness, while daunting, is utterly separate from the cynicism that marks his public life. As a rule I don't do this sort of thing anymore. But I also maintain that the hit man's trade is, well, if not honorable at least necessary. The kid-gloves politeness of "responsible" journalism is also necessary, of course, but there's no denying that it's part fraud, conveying deference when even the legit journalist privately believes none is due. A good hit man can lift the veil, blow the whistle, prick the balloon (and mix the metaphors).

Our patron saint is the great Mencken. In the first of his books to sell widely, *Prejudices: First Series*, he set the standard that all may aspire to and none attain. The objects of his attacks made up a catalogue of respectable figures: from Bernard Shaw to Thorstein Veblen, William Allen White to Joyce Kilmer. All were revered as a matter of etiquette by the genteel press of their time, as, for example, Walter Cronkite is today. And most, like Cronkite, were utterly vacant men. Mencken's most outrageous hits did not spring, as some of his apologists say, from a fierce sense of outraged propriety. He wasn't moralizing. He was having fun. When he composed his famous tribute to William Jennings Bryan ("a charlatan, a mountebank, a zany without sense or dignity"), he was delighting in the rapture that seizes a man when he is saying something that no one else dares say and that, upon reflection, is almost certainly true.

I think we need more of this, not less—no matter the hand-wringing from the Annenberg School and the Freedom Forum, and other sloughs of fretfulness. Although the best hits are written for the sheer joy of contrarianism, they do incidentally perform a public service, by encouraging skepticism toward the vast edifice of backscratching and flattery that journalism helps construct. If the fretters will come across with a grant, I could easily produce a monograph on how to proceed. Once again Mencken serves as guide. For a hit to be successful, the bile should be genuine and unforced. Its corrosive effects should expose not merely the subject's vacancy but also some larger sham. Motive-mongering is forbidden, as are details of the subject's personal life. Aim, of course, should be taken at public figures only, the more honored the better—Mort Zuckerman is suitable, the poor saps who collect rent checks for him are not. And journalists themselves should not be excluded from the category of deserving targets—especially if they are more prominent and better paid than I.

I can hear the Annenberg fellows now: What about civility, the integrity of public discourse? And what about the wounded feelings? My own view is that there's civility aplenty around already, surely enough to withstand a little more nastiness in public discourse. As for the wounded feelings, we should bear in mind the impenetrable vanity that girds most public figures. Kinsley tells a story about Charles Wick, the former director of USIA whom Kinsley had once called a "jackass." Long after the column appeared, Wick invited him to lunch. "I'm glad," Kinsley said, after Wick paid the check, "that you don't hold it against me that I once called you a jackass." To which Wick made the deathless reply: "I don't mind criticism from the press, if it's fair." So long as colossi like Charles Wick bestride the earth, we hit men will always find work.

Next Question, Please

April 1993

ANDY WARHOL'S OVER-QUOTED REMARK—IN the future everyone will be famous for fifteen minutes—may not be true for the wider world, but I'll lay even money it holds true for Washington, where I live. By the turn of the century, I predict, every Washingtonian will be momentarily famous, because by then every Washingtonian will have appeared on C-SPAN.

With its cameras trained on our elected representatives, C-SPAN is an unquestioned advance in American democracy, the greatest boon to self-government since the Fifteenth Amendment. But with its televised news conferences, journalist roundtables, viewer call-ins, live coverage of think-tank chin-wags, C-SPAN is also a yawning, bottomless maw with an insatiable hunger for talking heads. As a consequence, it has steadily inflated the ranks of those who consider themselves pundits. It's like an entitlement program without means-testing.

I am proof of the phenomenon, having been a guest on C-SPAN a dozen times or more without having any specific reason for being there. This, in fact, is a good working definition of the political pundit. Washingtonians and other political junkies have long lived among a class of people whose only job is to have opinions. We've gotten used to it, the way

7

we've gotten used to D.C.'s malarial summers or the hookers on Fourteenth Street. You have only to think of, say, Mark Shields fumbling through the intricacies of Slavic ethnicity, or John McLaughlin discoursing with Olympian certitude on the actuarial troubles of the Social Security system, to be reminded how implausible this line of work really is.

For myself, I assumed the mantle of pundit gingerly. Pleading stage fright, I resisted my first opportunity, in 1986, to appear on a C-SPAN viewer call-in show. But my employers— I was working at *The American Spectator*—felt obliged to insist, citing unspecified PR benefits. I failed to see how the nationwide exposure of a petrified junior editor would enhance the magazine's reputation. I lost the argument and did the show, though I eventually left the magazine. (Its circulation has since tripled.)

That first show was broadcast from our offices on a roaring hot summer morning. The air-conditioning had failed the night before. Brian Lamb, the gentlest and hence the most deceptively effective of interviewers, nudged me and my fellow panelist through the first damp half hour. After a shaky start I managed to thread my way through questions on the causes of homelessness, the ideological coloration of the *Washington Post*, the future of journalism, and several other subjects about which I knew next to nothing. I had almost found my bearings when Lamb turned to the phones.

An aggressive voice thundered over my earpiece: "I've got a question for Mr. Ferguson!" The videotape shows me rise a half inch from my chair, sending a spray of sweat toward the camera. The voice went on: "Last night ABC showed a movie about the Vietnam War, and they proved that the Pentagon shipped some of our boys back in body bags that had the wrong names on them." I stared at my trembling hands. "And what I want to know is," boomed the voice, "what is Mr. Ferguson going to do about THAT?"

In the silence that followed I thought of my mother, who had always been so proud of me, and I thought of my girlfriend. Both were watching, of course, watching me color, watching my face tighten, watching me bob up and down as I pumped my thigh against the bottom of the table. "Mr. Ferguson?" Brian said at last, probing for signs of consciousness. I raised my eyes gravely toward the camera and lowered my voice. "War," I said, "is a terrible thing."

I like to think that Shields couldn't have done better. As we went to the next caller, I had a feeling of exhilaration, of invincibility—an inner strength I can now summon whenever that little light above the camera flickers on. Today I am a pundit.

My high-water mark in this part-time career did not come for a few more years. I had written a brief piece in *The American Spectator* anticipating the twenty-fifth anniversary of the assassination of John F. Kennedy. As it happens, I think Kennedy was a pretty good president—you may quote me— even though my knowledge of him, then as now, was what I had picked up from the cursory reading of a few books. But my article aimed to deflate, gently, what I assumed would be the worst sort of memorial puffery, which sure enough poured out in great billowing clouds as the anniversary approached.

The article was a contrarian exercise, typical of a young on-the-make journalist trying to draw attention to himself. Amazingly, it worked. Within a few days I got a call from a network correspondent who told me he'd read it (loved it!) and wanted me (me!) to sit for an interview on the subject of Kennedy's presidency. The interview was to be taped, after which it would be woven into a five-night series marking the anniversary. I said sure. So far had my descent into punditry progressed that I don't recall ever considering begging off.

"Now, you're sort of taking an anti-Kennedy position, right?" the correspondent said—instructed, actually—as he placed me in front of the cameras. "You bet," I said. The little light flickered on, the cameras rolled. We ran through half a dozen issues. The Cuban Missile Crisis? I thought hard, trying to remember something about the Cuban Missile Crisis. I emerged with the defiant revisionism of a Cold Warrior: JFK had caved to Khrushchev, I said darkly, by guaranteeing Castro's sovereignty and dismantling missiles in Turkey (I hoped to God it was Turkey) in return for a concession that wasn't really a concession. Civil rights? I swung left, averring that Kennedy had been timid in the face of a historic moral opportunity. On the character issue, I veered right again, sounding like Jimmy Swaggart before they found him in that motel in Baton Rouge.

I enjoyed myself hugely. When we were through, the host walked me to the door. "Great!" he said. "Fabulous! You really know your stuff!" I don't think he was kidding.

Unfortunately, I never got to see the series, but several friends told me about it. There, evening after evening, into millions of American living rooms marched a parade of Kennedy experts: Kennedy historian Arthur Schlesinger, Jr., Kennedy butt boy Richard Goodwin, Kennedy speechwriter Ted Sorensen, Kennedy reporter Hugh Sidey, and . . . me. As they extolled the fallen president's mastery of statecraft, I popped up as equal time, the turd in the punch bowl. Since I haven't seen the tape, I don't know which of my quotes were used, but I do know this: they were provocative, succinct, and uncompromising. It's my job.

Nixon's Nemeses

May 1993

FOR ALL ITS BLESSINGS, AFFLUENCE CARRIES a curse: the creation of entire classes of people who don't, as a technical matter, have any reason for being here. The golf pro, the anti-smoking activist, the Gestalt therapist— each forgoes productive employment to surf on the lagniappe of an economy that creates more wealth than it can properly dispose of. Some of these people are harmless or amusing; some are pests and parasites. Some are professors of journalism.

Cruising the quad, lost in labyrinthine and pointless thought, J-school profs lead a professional life of astounding implausibility. Their object of study is not the mystery of the material universe or the enduring ideas of a faraway epoch but the fishwrap and birdcage-liner of the day before yesterday. Yet this irrelevance seems only to expand their capacity for mischief. Eager youngsters seek them out for professional training, while the news industry showers them with subsidies, underwriting the production of pamphlets, studies, surveys, and monographs—all the grim paraphernalia that flatters newspaper editors into believing their daily grind really is worthy of scholarly attention, even if they have to pay for it themselves.

It is an incestuous marriage, this coupling of editors with the academics who study them. I came upon one of their offspring the other day, a study called *Ways with Words*, produced under the auspices of the American Society of Newspaper Editors and presented at this year's ASNE convention. ASNE conventions are, by tradition, devoted exclusively and in equal measure to six topics: how to hire more blacks in the newsroom, more Latinos in the newsroom, more women in the newsroom, more Aleuts in the newsroom, more gays in the newsroom, and how to reverse the decline in newspaper readership by appealing to more blacks, Latinos, women, Aleuts, and gays.

Ways with Words is addressed to this last concern, though it downplays matters of race, sex, and tribal affiliation. Worries about declining readership have obsessed the newspaper industry since—well, since journalism professors were hired to study declining readership. Now a note of panic is creeping in. The study's authors conjure up a desperate premise: newspapers today are too darned smart for their own good. "Our journalism," they write, "seems to be just beyond the grasp of far too many Americans." The study thus suggests ways to dumb down newspaper writing, in hopes of finding the perfect coincidence between the stupidity of the people who consume newspapers and the cynicism of the people who produce them.

To aid in the effort, the authors enlisted the *St. Petersburg Times*, a paragon of the modern American newspaper. Staffed exclusively with J-school grads, the *Times* is graphically sumptuous, festooned with Pulitzers, and unreadable. The paper was used for this experiment: Each day, for four days, a news event was written up in four different styles; each story was placed in a different edition, and readers of each edition were then polled to discover their reactions.

The academics and newsfolk, in other words, went to a great deal of trouble, and you won't be surprised to learn that it wasn't worth it. *Ways with Words* reproduces the four versions of the four stories, and reading through them—I want to be candid—I fell asleep not once but twice. The stories had to do with subjects as various as suffering pets and shoreline development, and each version was uninteresting in its own way. I suspect the academics who assembled the study nodded off, too. They dutifully concocted some "statistically based path analysis" charts, to show "cause-and-effect relationships among factors," but this summation speaks, I think, for us all: "We learned there are no easy answers; neither are there alternatives to finding the tough ones."

You can almost see the gentlemen (and women) of the ASNE pat their tummies and shout: "Hear, hear!" The newspaper industry has become a timid, inbred enterprise—notwithstanding its long-overdue outreach to the Aleut community—and *Ways with Words* proves the point. Asking journalism professors to help improve newspaper writing is like asking the arsonist to put out the fire. Newspapers, through grants and subsidies and closed hiring practices, created America's journalism schools; and now J-schools, through their graduates, have re-created America's newspapers. The result has been the steep decline in newspaper quality, which in turn has resulted in the decline in newspaper readership, which newspapers then hire journalism professors to study. Talk about cause-and-effect relationships among factors!

Still, the blame for America's unreadable newspapers must lie with the professional newsfolk, not the profs who feed off them. Several years ago, at an ASNE convention in Washington, I heard the harshest, and truest, assessment of the industry from an expert in the field—Richard Nixon. At one plenary session, Nixon delivered, without notes, a talk breathtaking in its knowledge and originality. The editors gave him a standing ovation. As he left the ballroom, I told him I never thought I'd see a roomful of newspaper editors give anyone a standing ovation, much less Richard Nixon. Nixon looked over his shoulder at the crowd. "Yeah, well," he said, shrugging. "They're still a bunch of shits."

Final Copy

September 1994

IT WAS ONLY A MONTH OR SO AGO, DURING vacation, that I became conscious of my love for the obituary.

Part of the pleasure of a vacation, in theory, is the sense of isolation it offers from the demands of a daily routine. This includes newspaper reading. And so on my most recent escape I ignored the national newspapers and relied solely and casually on the local paper. It was one of those sugary confections from the Gannett chain, with all the Gannett trimmings: lots of color, superb weather coverage, a finger-in-the-wind editorial page, and dozens of stories no longer than a paragraph—like *USA Today*, only not so highbrow.

None of which bothered me—I was, after all, on vacation. But after several days of this pleasant new routine (five minutes to read the paper!) I longed for something more. I didn't long for, say, the three-part series on the dangers of derivatives that was (I assumed) running in the *Wall Street Journal*, or the *Washington Post*'s six-parter on the roots of urban despair, or the *New York Times*'s exhaustive debunking of the opposition to affirmative action. I wouldn't have read those even if I weren't on vacation. What I missed, day by day, was finding out who was no longer with us, who had answered the Final Summons, who had joined the Choir Invisible, who had croaked. I missed the obituaries.

15

Naturally, my local sheet featured the death notices marching down the page in grim columns of agate type, and a brief citation or two of more prominent deaths at the top. This merely whetted my appetite, for what I missed specifically were the obituaries of the *New York Times*. Having tarted herself up over the last decade with lipstick and rouge and stiletto heels, the Old Gray Lady is of course no longer gray; she's no lady, either. From the national newspaper of record, the *Times* has devolved, as the journalist David Brooks has perfectly put it, into the local paper of the Upper West Side of Manhattan. Even so, she still does two things better than anyone else. The arts coverage, while often trivial, is more comprehensive than any other daily paper's, and the obits are simply out of this world.

Is my tone too racy for so somber a subject? The truth is that the obituaries are the liveliest page of the paper, surely the only page that can rouse any sense of anticipation in this veteran reader. Obituaries, said Joseph Epstein, are the only real news. Almost every other event described in the daily paper can be reversed, sooner or later. Elections can be recounted, regulations rescinded, acts of Congress withdrawn or revised; the soaring popularity of a movie star will evanesce by and by. Not so with death. Death (and I don't think I'm the first to have noticed this) is for keeps. In the particular instance it happens only once, giving it the charm of singularity; yet it happens to everyone, which guarantees a universal interest. It is news that stays news.

Within the journalism business itself, though, the art of the obituary is considered second-rank work. No one aspires to be an obituary writer. In fact, writers aspire to be anything but, for at most newspapers the obit desk is Siberia, or even (to press the Soviet metaphor) Lubyanka. The obit writer's professional standing is mercilessly described in John Ed Bradley's novel *Love and Obits*. Bradley's hero is a former feature writer for the *Washington Post* (here called the *Her-*

ald) whose rapid professional slide, greased by booze and sexual indiscretion, has terminated in obituary writing.

"The Obit desk, situated next to the ever-hectic copy aide station and the men's and women's toilets, occupied the least desirable bit of real estate on the entire fifth floor," Bradley writes. "Rather than banish the section to a far, dark corner, Cameron Yates, the paper's executive editor, stuck it a short distance from the elevators, as if to warn anyone entering the *Washington Herald* that this was the fate of those who failed him." The desk is manned by drunks, dawdlers, has-beens. The only residue of ambition belongs to the hero, who keeps story ideas hidden away in his desk drawer, against the day when he can again practice *real* journalism.

But what kind of journalism could be more real than obituaries—what story could be grander than the whole span of a man's life, seen at the very moment the curtain falls? One who was refreshingly undefensive about the obit writer's calling was Alden Whitman of the *Times*, rightly considered the father of the modern obit. Whitman transformed the *Times*'s notices from, as he put it, "a recording of a death" into a "recapitulation of a life." In the mid-1960s Whitman also began the somewhat ghoulish practice of seeking out prominent people for retrospective interviews, so as to flavor the obits with the subject's personality, while the personality was still twitching. If nothing else, it gets the obit writer out from behind that desk near the men's room.

Whitman even published a collection of his obituaries, *The Obituary Book*, in 1971. He was happy in his work, and the obits were full of swagger and bounce. In his hands they could become one or another of many things, proving the resiliency of the form: an occasion for reminiscence, a score-settling recollection of slights and grievances, a quiet celebration of the small or half-forgotten. Whitman's own politics were starkly left-wing, and they shone through every time he eyed the cooling body of a departed pol. In fact, *Times* obits today are often called out for their bias, political and otherwise. I suppose purists could thus trace to Whitman one origin of a larger corruption at the *Times*—the loss of "objectivity," the saturation of every news column with political bias. Fair enough. But for obituary lovers the Whitman approach is far more engaging than the *Who's Who* recital of the traditional death notice. My own obit for him would be a rave.

And who, to consider a final question, are these obituary lovers? Apparently we are legion. Newspaper experts tell me that the obit page is still the page of the paper most widely read, particularly in the provinces. The curiosity of this should be plain. For the obits are also the page in which, to judge by my recent sojourn to the provinces, such papers invest very little. Once again the tragicomedy of contemporary newspaperdom plays itself out in miniature: The industry pumps vast resources into color printing and accelerated delivery and electronic databases and sophisticated news analysis, to answer in ever more sophisticated ways the complex questions of an ever more sophisticated readership; the reader, meanwhile, fumbles past the color photos and the statistical nuggets to find the page that will answer the most pressing, and perhaps least sophisticated, question of them all: So who died?

A *People* Person

March 1993

I AM ONE OF THOSE FOLKS BARBRA STREISAND
sang about so dramatically, the people who read *People*.
Each Tuesday my issue arrives, under my wife's name, and
I gobble it up like a giant éclair, in private, in wolfish gulps.
Having done so I do not feel, pace Barbra, like the luckiest
people in the world. In fact I feel sort of dazed, as though I
had just been pummeled at high velocity by hundreds of thousands of tiny marshmallows.

Perhaps you think I'm slumming. I am not slumming. I
do not disdain *People*; I love it. In a pop culture suffused in
irony, fevered by cleverness, *People* is dead to irony, immune
to cleverness. I love its reassuring predictability, its knack for
reducing everything to the same level of inconsequence. In my
current issue, for example, the death of the Resistance fighter
who hid Anne Frank's family is noted alongside the an-
nouncement that Alex Trebek and his lovely wife are expecting their second child. Birth and Death, the renewal of Life:
It's like, you know, the Great Mandala.

People people know that each issue, from front to back,
will be nearly identical to the one that preceded it. We do not
like surprises. As I write, this week's *People* features on its
cover a toothsome TV actress who has taken a new lover even
as she makes a startling comeback in a surprise hit series—

as distinguished from next week's issue, which will feature a toothsome country singer who has taken a new lover even as she makes a startling comeback with a surprise hit record— or Princess Di. But this week's issue does contain a surprise: a jarring note to rouse us from the pleasant catalepsy that *People* induces in its readers as part of a sacred compact.

On page 1, in the space usually reserved for a publisher's note, we find instead a "letter" from *People*'s managing editor. It takes the form of a tribute to the magazine's founding managing editor, Richard Stolley, on the occasion of his retirement. In such circumstances overstatement is forgivable: Memorial prose, said Malcolm Muggeridge, is always noteworthy for its "prevailing flavor of syrupy insincerity." The problem here, though, is not insincerity but sincerity; there is little doubt that the letter means what it says.

Mr. Stolley is praised, as he should be, for founding *People*. But he is praised for even more: We are told that he "all but single-handedly invented the genre of personality journalism." Lights flash, sirens sound. *Genre? Personality journalism? People* readers are entitled to blanch. All along, in blissful torpor, we have assumed we were reading gossip vetted by fact checkers and laundered by Time, Inc.'s lawyers. Gossip, in other words, delivered with a certain sobriety (all the pictures are in black and white), but gossip nonetheless: primped, plumped, and processed for the entertainment of all and the edification of none.

You could of course dismiss this high-toned talk as you would any instance of title inflation. Gossip left to amateurs remains gossip. In the hands of highly paid professionals, it intensifies, by means of genrification, into "personality journalism." I remember Ed Norton, the sewer worker on *The Honeymooners*, telling a pretty girl that his official title was "subterranean engineer." But Mr. Stolley wants more than to assume the title of genre-founder. *"People,"* he is quoted as saying, "made the responsible but unrelenting study of personality and behavior a legitimate and even essential part of American journalism." He uses the word "craft." It's like Henny Youngman citing Bergson in defense of mother-in-law jokes. Mr. Stolley even says this: "Someone once described *People* as having changed the soul of American journalism."

I want to know that person's name. It is a commonplace that the sphere of publishable "news" has greatly expanded since *People* first appeared. Subjects once considered private are now deemed worthy of public attention. And *People*, as chicken or egg, surely played a part. That does not mean, as the magazine's subterranean engineers seem to think, that they have thereby enlarged our store of truth. It would be interesting to compare one of *People*'s pieces of "personality journalism" with, say, a press release concocted by an MGM flack in the forties. The range of subject matter would be different, of course—the MGM flack would never have described his starlet's undying devotion to her bastard children. But in both pieces of writing, the amount of genuine information would be about the same—which is to say, almost none.

And that's just fine with me. *People* carries its own simple rewards, and not one of them involves the "unrelenting study of personality and behavior." In any case, the magazine will survive its brief dip into pomposity. We people who read *People* know what we like, and the editors like giving it to us; Say's law holds us both in its immutable power. Where else can I learn—to choose a random item from this week's issue—that Jane Seymour "is eager to quash rumors that she has an affinity for her leading men"? Quash, Jane! Quash, *People*! We hear you! That's the magazine I know and love, and they can't take that away from me.

My Night with Gennifer

May 1994

I SMELLED HER PERFUME. SHE SLID HER HAND into mine. Her blonde ringlets brushed my cheek as she reached up on tiptoes to give me a kiss.

"Thank you, Andy. Thank you so much," said Gennifer Flowers . . .

Maybe I should begin at the beginning.

So I'm sitting in my office on a Friday afternoon, minding my own business, when the phone rings.

"Hi," said a chirpy voice. "This is Pam [not her real name—I can't remember her real name]."

Pam, it turned out, is a producer for the *Rolonda* show. That is the show's real name. I can't blame you if you've never heard of it; I hadn't either.

"Listen," said Pam, "we're doing a very special show next Tuesday up here in New York, and we're wondering if you'd be interested in coming on."

"You bet," I said. I always recall something Gore Vidal once said: "Never pass up a chance to have sex or appear on television." If you add "or eat," you have, by the look of him, Gore Vidal's guide to life. And he's done okay.

"Our very special guest will be Gennifer Flowers," said Pam.

"I'm there," I said.

"Would that interest you?"

"I'm there."

"You'd have to spend the night up here, I'm afraid. We're taping pretty late."

"I'm there."

"You're kidding," said my wife.

"I think it sounds like a gas," I told her. "Gennifer Flowers! I'll be able to tell our grandkids about it."

"And then you're spending the night?"

"Well, not with her!" I went to the bathroom cupboard, where I keep my wedding ring, which I seldom wear because I've never been able to get it sized right. Honest. I put it on with a flourish. "See?" I said. "I'll wear this the whole time."

"That didn't stop her before."

I'm still not sure why the *Rolonda* show called. All the producer told me was that I should be "anti-Clinton," which is no great stretch. From the "pro-Clinton" camp the show had booked Jacob Weisberg of *New York* magazine and Jane Furse of the *New York Daily News*.

Gennifer Flowers's appearance on *Rolonda* that Tuesday was to cap a day-long media blitz. She hoped to reintroduce herself to the American people, whom she believes formed an inaccurate picture of her during her first fifteen minutes of fame. She is, of course, the original Clinton "bimbo." When she leapt into the limelight, at a raucous press conference in January 1992, she presented audiotapes of conversations she'd had with then-governor Bill Clinton, which she said proved their intimate relationship.

The *Star* tabloid paid six figures for her story, and *Penthouse* reportedly paid even more for a nude layout.

Now she worries some people might have gotten the wrong idea. So she's marketing a complete set of the Gennifer-Bill tapes for $19.95—to dispel, once and for all, the impression that she's a gold digger.

I don't think she's getting very good advice.

Over the weekend I started to have second thoughts. Friends who'd seen *Rolonda* called it a "low-rent Sally Jessy Raphael," which is like calling someone "a fat Roseanne." At a party on Saturday, another friend told me the *Rolonda* producers had asked him to appear with Gennifer as well, but had then rescinded the offer. "I think they thought I wouldn't foam at the mouth enough," he said.

"Ah," I said.

Matters weren't helped along Tuesday morning, when the *Washington Post* ran a story about Gennifer's reemergence. They quoted her on Clinton: "His truth could set us all free." Not even Sidney Blumenthal has gone that far.

With my wife, I tried to keep up my enthusiasm. "You know what Gore Vidal says," I told her as she dropped me off at National Airport on Tuesday afternoon. "'Never pass up a chance to have sex or appear on television.'"

"Great," she said. "You can kill two birds with one stone."

At La Guardia, I was met by a car and driver—forty-five minutes late. In the studio they left me alone in the green room—with a tray of wilty cheese, stale crackers, and sliced chicken that practically screamed "salmonella." In time, a producer brought me to makeup. The makeup guy stared long and hard. He placed his hands on his hips. "This is going to take some work," he said.

Another producer told me I had to be kept separate from Gennifer, and from Jacob and Jane, before the show. He didn't want to destroy the "spontaneity" of our appearance. Gennifer would be given the bulk of the hour, he said, and then we journalists would be brought on for the final segment.

"Let's see some fireworks out there," he said. "Remember, we hope you'll be very conservative—very anti-Clinton."

"Well," I said.

A look of terror crossed his face. "You *will* be very conservative, won't you?"

"If you'd like."

He beamed. "Great. And very pithy. We like pithy."

I watched most of the show from the green room. Rolonda, an attractive woman in a tight miniskirt, sandbagged Gennifer without mercy.

Gennifer responded with surprising poise. Her southern accent had almost disappeared. Except for the excess of jewelry, she carried herself like a tax attorney. When her motives were questioned, she said: "Rolonda, I'm doing this for me. It's time I spent some time on Gennifer."

I thought this was a stroke of genius—the all-purpose, Me Decade rationale that Rolonda, Sally Jessy, Oprah, and their audiences usually swallow whole.

Maybe she's getting better advice than I thought.

At last they brought me to the studio. During a commercial break, Jacob, Jane, and I joined Gennifer in chairs on the stage.

Jacob pointed at me. "He's on your side," he told Gennifer.

"Thank God," she said. "I'll tell you, whoever said the truth will set you free was full of shit."

"I think that was Jesus," I said, but I don't think she heard me. I scanned the audience. An old fellow twisted a pinky in his ear. A dozen old ladies sat perfectly erect, their handbags in their laps. There was a score of large, younger women in stretch pants, and a smattering of round-shouldered truants. The audience whooped, hollered, and applauded on cue. This wasn't a Mensa meeting here. This wasn't commencement day at the Sorbonne.

The show resumed. I got to say something to the effect that, after all the motive-mongering directed at Gennifer, people might want to listen to the tapes, which really aren't flattering to Bill Clinton. Gennifer nodded gravely.

Jane played her role with relish. She even brought up Paula Corbin Jones: "Anybody who thinks that's sexual harassment probably thinks Gennifer Flowers is a natural blonde."

Whoops! Hollers! Cut to a commercial!

Rolonda did a brief wrap-up, repeated Gennifer's 800 number, and the show was over. Almost.

As the technician undid our microphones, Gennifer leaned across me to Jane.

"You listen up," she hissed. Her accent had suddenly returned. "You ever take a cheap shot like that at me again and I'll walk over there and knock your ass out of that chair so fast you won't know what happened."

Jane blinked.

"I have *never* pretended to be a natural blonde," Gennifer continued. "But if you want to talk about what's real, I'll tell you this: *My tits are real.*"

She stood up, gave a cold shoulder to Jacob and Jane, and paused in front of me. I could smell her perfume . . . But you already know this part.

And then Gennifer Flowers was gone.

"I have to call my wife," I said to no one in particular.

Saying It with Flowers

June 1995

IF I HAD A BETTER IDEA OF WHAT IT MEANT, I
might use the word "frisson" to describe the sensation I got
reading a sexually explicit book and coming across my own
name. "Startled" might be a better word; "freaked out" also.
At the time, though, none of these words leapt to mind. What
leapt to mind, and what I said, was, "Holy s——!" (And if
you think it's easy pronouncing those dashes, just try it.)

The sexually explicit work in question is *Passion and Betrayal*, the account by Gennifer Flowers of her long dalliance
with Bill Clinton, who until very recently was president of the
United States. I am but a minor character in their saga. In
its pages I never appear undressed, never take drugs, never
fear for my life. My body is not racked by heaving sobs, nor
does it tingle from head to toe with a passion unlike any I had
ever experienced. These activities are undertaken only by the
main characters, Miss Flowers and her erstwhile beau, and
they are recounted, as if you couldn't guess, in exquisite detail.
Would you like to know the nickname of the presidential
penis? Do you hunger to learn what color of lingerie makes
our commander in chief stand up and salute? How about the
First Lady's interest in bilateralism? Then *Passion and Betrayal* is the book for you.

27

It is not, however, the book for me, and this puts me in a
pickle, for as Miss Flowers's lubricious memoir is passed from
one gasping reader to the next my name will be inextricably
tied to hers. All journalists, as frustrated *artistes*, crave im-
mortality. Now that I've got it, it turns out to be not at all what
I had in mind. And in truth the fault is mine alone. My one
encounter with Gennifer Flowers occurred about a year ago,
when a daytime TV talk show—nationally syndicated!—
asked me and two other magazine types to appear with her.
At the time she was busy marketing a series of audiotapes of
phone calls she had recorded between herself and Bill Clinton.
We journalists were brought in to cast a world-weary gaze
over Gennifer's claims and render our professional judgment.
As it happened, I was the only one who gave them any cre-
dence—or as she puts it, rather too simply, "took her side."

"When it comes to reporting stories like mine," Miss Flowers writes in a reflective moment, "the mainstream media in
this country has [*sic*] shown supreme arrogance." But not
me! *She likes me.* On the TV show, she continues, "Andrew
Ferguson of the *New York Times* [*sic, sic, sic*—I'll get to this
later] was given about 15 seconds to make his case, and was
able to make an excellent point." That's just Gennifer, being
kind. It's true those fifteen seconds flew by, but my point
wasn't really so excellent, and I won't bother to repeat it here.
But I will make a couple of other points, which I think are
excellent, by way of correcting the record and clarifying, for
all time, my role in the life of a woman who has published a
book that contains not only my own name but also the line,
"I had turned my breasts into hand puppets!" (exclamation
in original).

First, I don't think I really have taken Gennifer Flowers's
side in her tiff with Bill Clinton. How long the affair lasted,
who said what when, who broke up with whom, how much
Hillary knew or cared—these are questions best left to the
interested parties themselves, and upon them I remain firmly

agnostic. Second, I have never worked for the *New York Times;* and now, of course, I never will. Third, I am made uneasy by being included, as Gennifer's text might be construed as doing, in a group she calls "the precious few"—that hardy band of courageous supporters who have never failed her. As she tells us elsewhere, "Precious" is the nickname for her genitals. I am a married man.

For now, anyway. My wife has read the relevant parts of *Passion and Betrayal,* without incident. But it is as a father, rather than a husband, that I am most concerned. Though stonewalled by the press, the book is in wide circulation, in a kind of samizdat, within the anti-Clinton community—a community that has come to include all of the North American land mass with the exception of a few precincts on the Upper East Side of Manhattan and the entire town of Brookline, Massachusetts. My son is close to school age. Kids are cruel and taunting, as we know, and worse, they never get the story straight. With suffocating dread I await the day, surely not long from now, when my beautiful boy comes to his father after a rigorous working over from the bullies in the schoolyard, and with eyes wide as saucers pops the deadly question: "Daddy, is it true you went on TV and pretended a lady's breasts were puppets?"

Fools' Names, Fools' Faces

Low Profiles

November 1995

IF YOU PICKED UP OCTOBER'S *GQ* MAGAZINE, the one with John Travolta on the cover, you probably assumed, reasonably enough, that you could read an article about John Travolta if you wanted. You would have been only half right. That is indeed Travolta on the cover, hips jutting, fingers splayed, tongue glistening, a Creature from a Seventies Black Lagoon. And yes, over there on page 182, that is an article with the name "John Travolta" in the headline. But the truly important words are just below: "By Tom Junod." Junod is a writer-at-large for *GQ*, and a gifted one, but if you want Tom Junod to tell you about John Travolta, you're going to get an earful about Tom Junod, too. And if you don't like it, you can go buy another magazine with John Travolta on the cover.

Not that it would make much difference. All the upscale mass-circulation magazines seem to suffer from the same malady these days, whether *GQ*, *Vanity Fair*, *Esquire*, or any other of the "slicks." Their production values are uniformly high, their pages so fragrant and thick and luscious it's all you can do to keep from slurping them into your mouth; but reading them is a less appealing option. In particular, the celebrity profile—always a staple of this market—has fallen on hard times, a victim of the self-referential journalist of the 1990s.

Junod's article begins with John Travolta giving Tom Junod a dancing lesson. More precisely, the star is teaching the writer how to duplicate the walk Travolta perfected in *Saturday Night Fever.* "I tried walking like John Travolta," Junod writes. "I tried swinging my arms. I tried rolling my shoulders. I tried . . ." and so on. Nothing works. Junod worries that his hips aren't loose enough; he confesses that his testicles don't swing as they're supposed to. Poor Tom Junod is having a heck of a time—as is the reader, who is 250 words into the story and has yet to read much of anything about John Travolta.

Skip to the top of the next section of the Travolta profile. "I told him a sad story," Junod writes, "and he cried." Here at last is some solid information: John Travolta cries easily. Suddenly, in print, Junod offers the reader a gusher of data: The star likes iced tea, seldom drinks alcohol, often orders three desserts at a time, and uses the word "pee-pee." Then the pace of the story slows. and we're back to business—back to Tom Junod. "If John Travolta can do what he does because he is so big," Junod wonders, "then does that make everyone else . . . namely me . . . sort of, um, small?"

This is the theme Junod wrestles with for the duration of the story. At its close we read: "I had interviewed him about his life, his childhood, his acting, his comeback [alas, none of this material made it into the article], and yet the interviews were never about him—somehow they were always about me. . . ." Perhaps you thought John Travolta was a famous movie actor, or a faded cultural icon, or a former sex symbol reestablishing himself as a character actor in several hit movies. And so he may be. For *GQ* readers he is something more: He is an occasion for Tom Junod to think and write about . . . Tom Junod.

The self-referential celebrity profile is a new twist in the annals of show biz journalism. For decades, reporting on movie stars was merely an adjunct to a movie studio's larger public relations apparatus. Back in the thirties or forties, a *Photoplay* profile of, say, Joan Crawford might show the psychotic star surrounded by her beleaguered children, but Mom would look loving, and the kids would look happy, and MGM's photo department would have taken care to airbrush the cigarette burns from their little scalps. A squib on Errol Flynn's visit to a Hollywood High football practice would neglect to mention that he was trying to seduce the quarterback. Of course, we are not allowed to think that our present-day journalists would be a party to duping the public in this way. Journalists today are skeptical, hardheaded; they afflict the comfortable. They have learned the lessons of Vietnam, and of Watergate. They speak truth to power.

They are not, however, above consoling the subjects of their profiles, so long as it places them at the center of the action. Last spring, Kevin Sessums of *Vanity Fair* unfurled a long narrative about the ingenue Meg Ryan. The profile began, as profiles usually do nowadays, *in medias res*, with Kevin escorting Meg around downtown Savannah, Georgia. She's hungry; he feeds her. They discuss a book about Savannah they've both read: She didn't like it; he did. A rapport is established. Sessums is too modest to come out and say it, but it's pretty clear that Meg Ryan thinks Kevin Sessums is okay—more than okay. Before long she is telling him about her estranged mother, "speaking out for the first time about the situation." A scoop!

After twenty or so paragraphs, Sessums sits down for a heart-to-heart with Dennis Quaid, Meg's husband, and tells him that he's very moved by the two of them. Before the reader can gauge Quaid's reaction, the scene shifts. Now Sessums is talking to Meg again, about Quaid's cocaine addiction. He is careful to render his own observations verbatim. Sessums writes: "'Cocaine may harden one's heart, but it makes one, well, less hard in other places,' I venture. 'If you were intimate with him, how could you not know he was snorting coke?'" Meg's answer is less important than the question itself, and the fact that Kevin asked it at all. The message is unmistakable. Not just any journalist—not just any guy—can sit down with a gorgeous movie star and ask her point-blank about her husband's erections. Is it any wonder that by the end of the story, Kevin is feeding Meg *again*?

"I place the sweet potato pie on the kitchen counter," he writes. And once more he assumes the journalist's burden.

"'Do you pray?' I ask her."

From sex to God: This is a tough interviewer.

"She begins to sob. 'I'm sorry—I haven't . . .' The tears won't stop.

"'Are you O.K.?' I ask, crossing the room to where she has sunk into a sofa and holding her until she can regain her composure."

With Meg safe in Kevin's arms, the story deliquesces to a gentle close. She does regain her composure. And then they dig into that sweet potato pie. Just the two of them. Kevin and his movie star.

It is important to stipulate here, in the interests of fairness, that Sessums's self-references—like Tom Junod's, like the dozen other instances that appear monthly in the slicks—are wholly unnecessary. They add nothing to a reader's knowledge of the celebrity being profiled, and I cling to the conviction that readers are drawn to a movie-star profile because they want to know about the movie star and not the journalist. (Why anyone would care to read about Meg Ryan or John Travolta in the first place is a separate mystery.)

Of course, for the journalist the self-referential technique has its uses. It makes the unpleasant task of constructing a narrative infinitely easier. "Carly greets me at the door," writes Marie Brenner in a *Vanity Fair* profile of Carly Simon. "We are not strangers." And so it goes: "One morning Carly telephones me, saying. . ." "When Carly and I sit down for our first interview. . ." "One evening Carly telephones me, saying. . ." It is an impeccably postmodern device. The celebrity profile becomes a story of a writer trying to write a celebrity profile.

The technique also, most deliciously, lends itself to self-aggrandizement, a quality prized by all writers. In the March *Esquire*, Bill Zehme wrote a profile of Sharon Stone that revealed some data about the star, but none so important as the fact that Bill Zehme is one of her pals. He has ridden in her car. He has cooked with her. He has met several of her beaux. And, hold on to your hat, he has gotten a massage with her. "I have lain naked with her," he wrote in the story's lead paragraph, "only because she insisted, only because other people were present, only because I could tell you about it." Telling us about it, actually, is the point. We learn relatively little about Sharon Stone, but the average *Esquire* reader—that unhappy fellow who's still trying to get his new suspenders to look like they do in the Perry Ellis ad—that guy surely comes away thinking that Bill Zehme is one lucky dude.

But there is more going on here even than this—more, even, than the poignant spectacle of puppyish hacks nuzzling up against movie stars in hopes that the glamour rubs off. Consider the situation the poor writer finds himself in. People become writers because they want to draw attention to themselves. To a man (or woman), they're egomaniacs. And at last they've met professional success. A slick magazine is paying them big money. And then to be confronted by a vacuum-with-legs like . . . *Keanu Reeves* . . . or *Brad Pitt* . . . or *Nicole Kidman*. And these nullities, these pouty-lipped *zeroes*—the writer has to make them interesting! Even the most starstruck journalist would much rather write about something of intrinsic interest: "namely me," as Tom Junod puts it. So he does.

* * *

A final question remains: Why do editors let them get away with it? The answer lies in the dimmest past, in New Journalism, the profoundly influential "movement" begun in the early 1960s. Tom Wolfe wrote the genre's manifesto, in 1973, with a good humor that just skirted the edges of pomposity. New Journalism, he said, was "the first new direction in American literature in half a century." New Journalists "penetrated the lives of their characters," just as the great realist writers of American fiction had done. The journalist of tomorrow would abandon the stale constraints of old journalism and fashion his reportage into narratives by means of techniques heretofore known only to novelists: dialogue, scene-setting, the accumulation of status detail, and, most trickily of all, their characters' point of view. Thus could a journalist re-create, with unprecedented vividness, events he may not have seen himself.

With Wolfe and his colleagues, magazine journalism changed forever. The word went forth—a bacillus cratering through the journalism schools, infecting the ranks of aspiring freelance writers, all of them unaware that there was one minor problem with New Journalism: Not many people could pull it off. Hardly anybody, in fact. Done right, it required the rarest combination of gifts: heroic reporting skills on the one hand, and, on the other, a technical mastery found only in superior literary artists.

You don't hear much about New Journalism anymore. It survives only in its decadent phase—as an influence, an indulgence, an excuse, a license, a husk of Wolfe's lofty ambitions. All celebrity profiles these days set scenes—whatever scenes the writer happens to have been in. All include dialogue—whatever the writer said to the celebrity, and vice versa. And all of course are drenched in point of view—the writer's. And it is, almost without exception, a point of view that is stupefyingly banal.

Here, then, is what remains of "the first new direction in American literature in half a century." We are left with such scenes and dialogue as this, from Scott Raab's profile of the sleazeball movie star Mickey Rourke, in a recent *GQ*:

I ask him about [a] 16-year-old supermodel.
"I would not go near a 16-year-old girl. I don't even fuck. I've gotta be in love to fuck a woman. I'll get a blow job, but I cannot fuck unless I'm in love."
"Me neither," I say. "How about a blow job?"
"Open it up," Mickey says, laughing, pointing at my crotch . . . My zipper stays closed.

Well, thank God. Writers have to draw the line somewhere.

From the Mouth of Babs

March 1995

A WEEK AFTER SHE DELIVERED HER LECTURE "The Artist as Citizen" to Harvard's Kennedy School, the headline in *People* was unapologetic: "Lampoon her if you like, feisty Barbra Streisand draws rave reviews and a full house at Harvard."

I know all about lampooning leftist movie stars. You can't cover politics in Washington without bumping up against them, and I've so enjoyed the experience I've made it a hobby. The result is a satchel of memories with which I hope someday to dazzle my grandchildren, assuming my grandchildren will be dazzled that Grandpa once got hugged by Jon Voight. But that's not all. Cher asked me my name during a press conference. Glenn Close once squeezed my hand. And, unforgettably, I spent forty-five minutes—I mean, *forty-five minutes*—listening to Susan Dey excoriate the Bush administration for cutbacks in the HUD budget. I could have drowned in her eyes.

Much as Democrats appreciate their efforts, the stars sometimes find themselves in over their heads. Several years ago, a planeload of stars was flown in for a pro-abortion march on the Washington Mall, and when they disembarked, a publicist brought me over to interview a gorgeous TV starlet. I asked her the usual question about why she was here, expecting the usual invocation of "back-alley abortions" and coat hangers. She gave an empty glance to the PR guy, who nodded encouragement. "Well," she said, "I wanted to join the march because of my commitment to all human life. All life is sacred, even the life of the un . . ." Gorgeous or not, this one had been badly briefed! The publicist whisked her away in mid-sentence to a corner of the press tent, where he gesticulated wildly. When she and I spoke later, she had got with the program. She talked about coat hangers with the confidence of a hat-check girl.

This is the kind of elementary mistake that Barbra Streisand would never make. She knows where she stands on the issues. As a Hollywood arm-twister she raises millions for the Democratic party. She is famously chummy with President Clinton, though probably less so with his wife. She sang for JFK and LBJ and has dined with Janet Reno. She sits on boards and stuff. Frank Rich, the left-wing attack dog of the *New York Times*, has dubbed her, with his typical accuracy, the only public defender of liberalism in America.

Hence her invitation to speak at the Kennedy School; hence her acceptance; hence "The Artist as Citizen"—though a better title, from the Kennedy School's perspective, would be "The Artist as Citizen with a Million Dollars to Donate to a Foundering School of Public Administration." Her road to this august podium was not smooth. The March number of *Vanity Fair* describes her split with Leon Wieseltier, *The New Republic*'s literary editor and the party's preeminent intellectual. Leon had called politically active stars "bubble-headed." (Lampoon them if you will!) "Such a negative, jealous, maybe not jealous, but mean-spirited attitude toward this generality of people!" Barbra responded.

Whether the Democratic party—already struggling for its soul—could have survived a permanent rift between its Wieseltierian and Streisandian wings, we will never know. For a rapprochement was devised by Shirley MacLaine, her-

self a Democrat. Together the warring philosophes watched
the movie *Quiz Show*, at Barbra's house, on the couch. "They
spoke each other's language," said Miss MacLaine. But we
already knew that.

Here, from "The A as C," is some of Barbra's language: "Art
is the signature of a generation." "After many years of self-
scrutiny, I've decided the most important things come from
outside myself." "I'm very proud to be a liberal, okay?" And,
implausibly: "There are reasonable Republicans." Barbra
swears she wrote the speech herself, but I detect here the weight
of Leon's learned hand. Surely they did more on that couch
than watch a lousy movie.

People is right: It is too simple to lampoon the artist as citizen. She should be seen in her natural habitat, so I rented the
new video *Barbra: The Concert*. Even here, alas, the adjec-
tive "bubble-headed" clings to her like a burr. Anyone who
has tried to forget her career will be shocked to discover that
her repertoire ("Evergreen," "The Way We Were," "You
Don't Bring Me Flowers") is just as annoying as it seemed on
first hearing. Her technique remains unchanged too. With her
cavernous sinuses, her inexhaustible lungs, she doesn't so
much sell a song as wrestle it to the ground and kneel on its
throat. She should try this with her songwriters.

The show is a two-hour valentine, self-addressed; narcis-
sism is the theme. The script has her reenact her therapy sessions. There are still more epigrams: "Relationships are difficult to have," she announces. (Leon's influence again.) And
in closing she says: "Take care of yourselves. And each other.
I'm really happy, I mean that," as if we were ever in doubt!
Her encore is "Somewhere": "Hold my hand and we're halfway there. Hold my hand and I'll take you there."

Of course she will. Here, then, is the Artist as Artist:
self-indulgent, sanctimonious, obtuse and frivolous and
over the hill. Barbra isn't merely the defender of modern liberalism. She is its symbol.

Sinatra at Eighty:
Scoobee-Doobee-Don't

December 1995

FRANK SINATRA TURNS EIGHTY ON DECEM-
ber 12, setting off one of those familiar convulsions in the vast
publicity machine of American show biz. The smoke has
barely cleared from the last such convulsion, concluded only
a week or two ago for the Beatles, on the twenty-fifth anniversary of their breakup as "the band that changed the
world." The juxtaposition makes for a revealing contrast. For
Frank never much liked the Beatles, never grew comfortable
with the way they changed the world. Of course he didn't: The
world they changed, back there in the mid-sixties, was Frank's
world.

And so now, thirty years on, we have the TV specials, the
CD retrospectives, the radio marathons, the somber appreciations in the newsmagazines and in the lifestyle sections of
newspapers. And books by the crateful, ranging from the
merely worshipful to the hagiographic. To choose one almost
at random: *Sinatra! The Song Is You*, a long and loving and
in many ways useful account of the singer's work by the critic
Will Friedwald, offers praise worthy of Bach or Shakespeare
or one of those guys, complete with terminology drawn from
Leo Strauss: "His artistic canon is as close to perfect as any
of us are able to deliver."

The self-described "saloon singer" has even inspired a "reader"—*The Frank Sinatra Reader*—a work that, unlike most other "readers," contains not a single word written by its eponymous subject. Piled one on top of the other, the tributes prove that, whatever art Sinatra may have produced himself, he has inspired some of the worst writing of the century. All right: I exaggerate. But it's catching. The novelist William Kennedy, asked to compose a tribute for Sinatra's seventy-fifth birthday, sets the tone: "In the 1950s, there came *In the Wee Small Hours*, which conditioned your life, especially with a young woman with lush blond hair who used to put the record on and pray to Frank for a lover. All that perfumed hair, and it came undone. That certainly was a good year. . . ."

The beatification of Frank Sinatra is upon us. But once you fan away the windy praise—"one of the three or four greatest interpretive artists the world has ever known"; "a body of work unrivaled in twentieth century music"; many other sentences that contain the word "oeuvre"—the tributes have their uses. They allow us to reconstruct Frank's world as it was before the moptops pushed him from center stage. And tell us why we should be forever grateful that they did.

The dicey task for Sinatra worshippers involves what is sometimes called the "Gauguin problem"—separating the brutishness of the artist from the beauty of his art. For Gauguin it was the cold-blooded ditching of his family for Tahiti, where he produced pictures of dangling fruit and overripe breasts; for Sinatra it was a "lifestyle" that entailed chronic misogyny, boozy brawls with pimps and whores, and lifelong social and business relationships with fellows named "The Weasel" and "Ratface." The lifestyle was chronicled with relish by Kitty Kelley in 1986's *His Way*, billed as an "unauthorized biography" but in fact an exhaustive catalogue of Frank's pathologies. One enduring image from Kelley's book—the image that sums up all that comes before and after—is of Frank in his Vegas suite after a show, late at night/early in the morning, knife and fork in hand, eating a hearty breakfast of steak and eggs—off the chest of a prostitute. He has always been a man of large appetites.

What better means to solve the Gauguin problem than a testament from the singer's loyal, grateful, parasitic daughter Nancy? Her coffee-table-sized *Frank Sinatra: An American Legend* inevitably recycles material from her earlier devotional memoir, *Frank Sinatra: My Father*, but it offers scant comfort for fans hoping to get past the mythic Sinatra vulgarity. The new book is a day-by-day chronicle of the Chairman's life, listing every gig at the Sands, every recording session, every Friars' roast of Dean and Sammy. And more: Here is Frank, offended at the gossip columnist Dorothy Kilgallen, sending her a full-sized tombstone with her name on it. Frank teaming up with Joe DiMaggio and a few "associates" to break down the door of an apartment where they suspected Marilyn Monroe was fooling around unsupervised. Frank, talking his "acquaintance" Sam Giancana into helping JFK "win" the West Virginia primary. Frank, denied credit at the baccarat table at the Sands, ripping the wires out of the switchboard and driving a golf cart through the lobby window. And this is the *authorized* biography.

Still, the daughter's natural protectiveness is endearing. When Frank travels to pre-Castro Havana to meet with Lucky Luciano, she is careful to say he "allegedly" had his picture taken. When she quotes one journalist on Frank's "alleged connections with mobsters," you can almost see her ball her fists: "It's obvious that Mr. Salerno had not done his homework, since my father had never been indicted for anything." A daughter's boast.

And yet, say Sinatra fans, and yet: There is, there will always be, the music, which they find mysteriously unspoiled by the personal shortcomings of the artist himself. *The Frank*

Sinatra Reader contains a number of essays supporting this view. Sinatra came to his greatest fame in the years following the war, when the nation's universities swelled with academics aching to apply their skills to the popular arts. As a consequence, he has probably had more baloney written about him than any other living American. The *Reader* offers a few of these efforts, but most of its critical appreciations of Sinatra the artist tend to be decidedly unacademic.

They tend, to the contrary, to be personal: some version, like William Kennedy's, of Sinatra and Me, in which the music seems less an independent artifact than an occasion to recapture lost youth. As Friedwald puts it: "So much of our lives have been lived to the soundtrack of Sinatra's [that] it's ultimately impossible to tell where our actual experiences end and those we've felt vicariously through Sinatra's lyrics begin."

Fine, as far as it goes, which isn't very far. Pop music of any time thrives on personal associations. Without them it loses much of its effect. A Beatles fan, contemplating the greatness of the band that changed the world, will almost inevitably end up remembering where he was when he first heard *Rubber Soul*, and then the Hendrix poster in his dorm room, and the incomprehensions of Mom and Dad. . . . This is one of the things that separates pop music from music that endures. Beethoven's appeal doesn't rest on your memories of making out in the back seat of your dad's Chevy while the radio played the Andante from the Emperor Concerto.

The problem arises when those associations are rolled out to make the case for the pop musician as Artist. Sinatra's greatest creative period, it's generally agreed, came in the 1950s, with the release of a series of albums on the Capitol label. "Being an eighteen-carat manic depressive," he once said, "I have an acute capacity for both sadness and elation." The Capitol albums are the perfect reflection of his either-or personality. They express one of two moods, exclusively. The big brassy albums, like *Songs for Swingin' Lovers*, show

Frank the swinger, with lots of shouted "Jacks" and "babes" thrown in for emphasis. The rest—the "suicide albums," like *Where Are You?* and *Only the Lonely*—show Frank in a funk, slumped against a lush, pillowy string orchestra that threatens to swallow him whole. Even for someone who neither danced nor made out to them, the albums have moments that force you to catch your breath. It's hard to imagine anyone listening to "I've Got You Under My Skin," from *Swingin' Lovers*, without getting giddy. And there are performances of surpassing delicacy: *Only the Lonely* closes with Johnny Mercer and Harold Arlen's great saloon song, "One for My Baby." In the forties, Friedwald tells us, Sinatra had sung the song in B. Here, though his voice has deepened and mellowed, he squeezes the key up to D. A piano plays in the distance; the strings, for once, are muted. The result is art of a heightened kind that popular entertainers seldom reach. It's almost enough to make you want to use the word *oeuvre*.

On the other hand . . . has any entertainer ever been cut so much slack by so many? Aside from Judy Garland? The suicide albums, with Frank's forced tremolo, his slides and funereal phrasing, are the work of a man for whom self-pity is the most pleasing indulgence. The mawkishness of, say, "I'm a Fool to Want You" from *Where Are You?* verges on self-parody. (Frank, get a grip!) Throughout the albums he hits more than a few notes flat, and they are preserved for the ages, an indelible part of the oeuvre. By many accounts, including his own, his legendary perfectionism seems indeed to have been just legend. As a recording artist he was in a hurry. "Often I was a little impatient in making a record," he said later, "and I said, 'That's it, press it, print it.'"

In extenuation for these lapses critics tend to overreach: Much is made of the conventions of the *bel canto* tradition, and technical terms like appoggiatura (a vocal slur) are desperately invoked. It doesn't wash. It should be no slight to Sinatra's formidable talent to point out that the phrasing so

celebrated by critics doesn't cut the best singing of Fred
Astaire, or that his tonal control and melodic sense can't
match those of the peerless Bing Crosby—neither of whom
has been celebrated in cults of Sinatraphiliac intensity.

The swing albums are similarly uneven. They are often
praised for their exuberance, but forty years later the exuberance just sounds like strut and swagger. Brassy, up-tempo versions of ballads like "They Can't Take That Away from Me"
and "Our Love Is Here to Stay" make you wonder whether
he's even aware of what the songs mean. Here the life really
does infect the art. It's not hard to imagine the Frank Sinatra
of the swing albums—the self-regarding, finger-snapping hip-
ster in the cocked fedora—finishing a recording session and
ordering up a hooker for a nice chestful of steak and eggs.

By the mid-1960s, the swinger Frank had atrophied into a
public persona. This was the Frank of the Rat Pack, trailing
greasy sycophants like Peter Lawford and Dean Martin and
Sammy Davis, Jr., the Frank of shot-on-the-fly movies like
Ocean's Eleven, of croaking, late-night shows in Vegas done
with a Camel in one hand and a glass of Black Jack in the other.
His greatest recordings receded into the distant past, as he
pushed unlistenable new product like "Strangers in the Night"
and (with Nancy) the aptly titled "Something Stupid." He was
seldom photographed out of a tux. Onstage he indulged his taste
for racist humor: "The Polacks are deboning the blacks. They
want to use 'em for wet suits." There were more brawls, more
vendettas against columnists who wrote unkindly. The life
overtook the art.

Worse, the life suffused the culture of American popular
entertainment. Most obviously there were the pale imitations
like Al Martino and Vic Damone, "class acts" with oil-can
pompadours and spit-shine shoes. Sinatraism sank to its
most attenuated form in the half-forgotten careers of Fabian
and Frankie Avalon and Bobby Darin, whose recording of

"Mack the Knife" is a *reductio ad absurdum* of the swingin'
Frank.

And then the Beatles arrived to sweep them all away.

The recent ABC special *The Beatles Anthology* broadcast that
famous first American appearance on *Ed Sullivan* in 1964.
From the opening notes of "All My Loving," the suffocating
oppressions of Sinatraism seemed to lift from all of show biz.
The Beatles were jaunty and smiling, with a gift for melodies
set to simple, unswinging beats, in songs they wrote themselves.
There was plenty of cockiness but no brooding. They joked with
the press. They didn't know anyone named "Momo."

Frank let it be known that the Beatles weren't his cup of
juice. Gay Talese's 1966 profile, "Frank Sinatra Has a Cold"
(included in the *Reader*), opens with a scene of intergenera-
tional ill will. The place is a Los Angeles drinking club. Sinatra
is feeling petulant; Sinatra often does. He is in the midst of
planning a TV special. The show's press release is written in
Sinatra-ese: "If you happen to be tired of kid singers wearing
mops of hair thick enough to hide a crate of melons, it should
be refreshing to consider the entertainment value of a video
special titled *Sinatra—A Man and His Music.*"

Frank leans against the bar, watching a group of young
men, psychedelically clad, playing pool. He isn't pleased. He
picks at one of them, the screenwriter of a new movie, *The
Oscar.* "I've seen it," Frank tells him, "and it's a piece of
crap." Before it's too late, Frank's "associates" escort the
young fellow from Frank's presence, and the Chairman of
the Board turns to the club manager.

"I don't want anybody in here without coats and ties," he
snaps. The manager nods and disappears, leaving Frank to
drink in peace.

There's a kind of poignancy in this vignette, a picture of a
man before the deluge. But as the 1960s wore on he gave in,

halfway. He appeared in Nehru jackets and gold chains, recorded songs, including Beatles songs, at soft-rock tempos, ordered up new toupees with bangs. He even married an exquisitely emaciated flower child, Mia Farrow, and let her travel to India (with the Beatles!) to sit at the feet of Maharishi Mahesh Yogi. In the supreme renunciation of his past he recorded an album of "sensitive" songs by . . . Rod McKuen.

In 1971 he threw in the towel, and retired. "He just feels his kind of show business era has ended," Nancy said at the time. As if to prove the point, he returned from retirement to an endless series of stints in Vegas and fly-in, fly-out stadium gigs—some solo, some with Dino and the Candyman, all enormously lucrative. His vast constituency remained loyal as it aged. He enjoyed a great hit with "New York, New York," whose chief virtue was that it replaced "My Way" as his signature song.

Sinatraism wouldn't die, but even after the Beatles broke up it survived among baby boomers merely as a ready-made joke. Bill Murray's lounge singer from *Saturday Night Live*—tuxedoed, tone-deaf, swingin' hard to the latest charts from Neil Diamond—was late-phase Sinatraism distilled to its essence. (Frank himself performed a number of Diamond's songs in the seventies.) The funniest piece ever written about Sinatra—funny pieces about Sinatra not being the biggest category in journalism—is Alex Heard's 1985 *New Republic* article, "Frankie and Ronnie," reprinted in still another commemorative collection, *Legend: Frank Sinatra and the American Dream*. Sinatra had just helped the Reagans celebrate the Inaugural in Washington, where he made a commotion by announcing to the assembled press: "You're all dead, every one of you. You hear me? You're all dead."

"Most Americans," Heard wrote, "have experienced that strange sensation produced by exposure to certain entertainers—a mixture of hatred, disgust, embarrassment, and pathos. Sometimes, if the performer is sufficiently schlocko or self-congratulatory, this feeling intensifies to a point at which, suddenly . . . it becomes highly pleasurable." Heard called the phenomenon "hathos," and ticked off a number of instances: "For many, watching Jerry Lewis 'take on his critics' in the waning hours of the Labor Day Telethon arouses this emotion; as does Sammy Davis Jr.'s Mr. Bojangles routine. . . . But for me, the chairman of the Hathos Board has always been none other than Old Rheum Eyes himself, Mr. Frank Sinatra."

The tragedy of artistic decline became farce. The baby boomers had made Frank a figure of fun.

What a difference a decade makes! Today Sinatra is everywhere. Last month an eightieth birthday celebration was held in Los Angeles, featuring tributes from Bob Dylan, Bruce Springsteen, Salt 'N Pepa, Paula Abdul, and Hootie *sans* Blowfish. ABC will broadcast the festivities two days after Frank's birthday. In the last two years he has released two albums of old standards, *Duets* and *Duets II*. Conceived by the rock producer Phil Ramone, they pair Sinatra with such contemporary stars as Luther Vandross, Gloria Estefan, Julio Iglesias, Carly Simon, and Bono from the rock group U2. As music the albums are toxic. As product they're platinum— double platinum, in fact, having outsold every other Sinatra release. In 1994 he was awarded an honorary Grammy for Lifetime Achievement, and Bono took the stage to introduce him, bestowing the imprimatur of Generation X: "You know his story because it's your story," Bono said. "Frank Sinatra walks like America: cocksure."

Compare this with another recent quote from another GenX idol, Michael Stipe of the band R.E.M.: "I've never sat down and listened to a Beatles record from beginning to end. Those guys didn't mean a fucking thing to me." The three-night, massively publicized ABC special *The Beatles Anthology* tanked in the ratings. It's no exaggeration to say that among people who matter—and in popular culture the people who matter are the youngest cohort of consumers with disposable income—Frank is hipper than the Beatles.

How to explain it? Unlike the Beatles, who are still close enough in time to be irony-proof, Frank can be kitsch—always a guarantee of big sales in our campy culture. One is reminded, too, of the old joke: Grandparents and grandchildren get along so well because they have a common enemy. Nothing could be more wounding for Beatlemaniacs than to hear their child announce that "Ring-a-ding-ding" speaks to him in a way that "Ob-la-di, Ob-la-da" does not. But the music itself is really beside the point. One of Sinatra's former arrangers, Billy Byers, has said, "*Duets* would be valid artistically if only the kids were learning to appreciate Frank Sinatra [the musician]. But they're not investigating other Sinatra albums." What they're investigating, and buying, is the Sinatra attitude, known now as Attitude. Generation Xers face the Gauguin problem their grandparents faced, only in reverse. For tastes shaped by Bono and Michael Stipe, *Songs for Swingin' Lovers* must be tough going. But with the Frank persona, they feel right at home.

As long ago as 1984, the rock writer Stephen Holden identified Sinatra as "a kind of proto–punk rocker, spitting at the world with pugnacious arrogance." Now *there's* a guy today's kids can look up to. Bono, in his uncontrolled way, finishes the thought: "Sinatra has got what we want: swagger and attitude. He's big on attitude. Serious attitude. Bad attitude. Frank's the chairman of the Bad. . . . I'm not going to mess with him. Are you?"

No, no. All that we can do—those of us caught in the middle, neither beatifiers nor detractors—is sit back and wonder at the durability, the resiliency, of Sinatraism, three decades after we thought it had been buried for good. It is once again Frank's world. We just live in it.

The Soft-Rock President

March 1993

AS IF BILL CLINTON DIDN'T HAVE ENOUGH problems, grumblings about his tenure are already being heard within the rock 'n' roll community. Members of the community, you'll recall, supported Clinton with an ardor matched only by the Esperanto-speaking and clothing-optional communities. His was supposed to be the first rock 'n' roll presidency, carried in on a euphoric wave of Arsenio and MTV, jokey allusions to Elvis, and a reunited Fleetwood Mac.

The Carter era had once held out the same promise—Willie Nelson, after all, smoked a joint with one of Jimmy's spawn on the White House roof. But Clinton seemed capable of so much more. The possibilities were breathtaking: Sting chanting tribal songs in the Rose Garden, Axl Rose terrorizing chambermaids in the Lincoln Bedroom, Ozzy Osbourne munching bats on the South Lawn. . . .

Now, alas, reality is settling in. The first discordant notes were sounded in *Rolling Stone*'s exhaustive coverage of the Inaugural extravaganzas. Community members bristled when lightweights like Michael Bolton and Kenny G took the stage and valuable airtime. "Just because Clinton can play the sax," groused a member of Megadeth, "doesn't mean he knows what rock 'n' roll is about." Another rocker was even more dismissive: "Bet Hillary Clinton likes James Taylor and Dan Fogelberg. Every victory has its price, folks, and this one's gonna make your head blow up."

I'm not certain what this last remark means, precisely, but the derisive tone is unmistakable. Members of the rock 'n' roll community, like members of all communities, can be difficult to please, but why, one wonders, are they so easy to surprise? To serious students of candidate Clinton, the rock affectations seemed as spurious as his devotion to a middle-class tax cut or Haitian refugees. The evidence was plain. At a campaign fundraiser, Barbra Streisand serenaded the candidate with a rendition of "The Way We Were"—a song that doctors who treat rock 'n' roll fans use routinely as an emetic. Yet, as Miss Streisand threw her head back and oozed out the melody, Clinton didn't flinch. He beamed. His eyes watered. *He mouthed the words.*

Even more definitive was an interview the candidate granted *People* last summer. Surveying the record collection in the governor's mansion in Little Rock, the interviewer asked Clinton "what album he would save if his house caught fire." After what must have been an interminable period of lower-lip biting, the governor replied: "That's a tough choice. [Aren't they all!] But if I had to take only one, it would probably be Judy Collins's *Colors of the Day.*"

As it happens, this album, though it was released in 1971, is still in print, available to any person who seeks a window onto our president's tastes—or who himself has a taste for 1960s folkie nostalgia. The cover shows Judy Collins at her most fetching, wandering a deserted beach, alone with her thoughts—the implication being that her thoughts are not small ones. The cover photo, in fact, is indistinguishable from a dozen others of the same vintage. Twenty years ago deserted California beaches were swarming with pop stars trying to get their cover photos taken as they wandered alone with their thoughts—Neil Young might trip over Richie Havens, who had just stepped on Joan Baez's foot, after she had backed into Joni Mitchell's photographer. This is one reason they all moved to Aspen.

Open *Colors of the Day*, and that distant time comes alive. On the inside cover, in a typescript familiar from Hallmark greeting cards, Judy Collins has reprinted a verse of her song lyrics, which also bears that special Hallmark touch:

> *What I'll give you since you asked*
> *Is all my time together*
> *Take the rugged sunny days*
> *The warm and rocky weather*
> *Take the roads that I have walked along*
> *Looking for tomorrow's time*
> *Peace of mind.*

The lines are indicative of the album's unvarying mood. Most of the songs are in a minor key, sparsely arranged, humorless, self-absorbed, skirting intelligibility. One tune stands out: "Farewell to Tarwathie," a sea chantey sung over a background recording of humpback whales. At the time, the song was considered an eloquent plea for the survival of the bulbous beasts. Today it seems almost designed to make an MTV viewer's head blow up.

It is a hard image to dislodge: the president of the United States, leader of the world's sole remaining superpower, listening late at night with eyes closed to the groans of humpback whales, echoing through the briny deeps. I doubt that *Colors of the Day* is much listened to anymore, outside the White House and those progressive college towns like Ann Arbor and Madison and Lawrence, where aging doctoral students sit cross-legged on futons in rental housing, sipping

Celestial Seasons and daydreaming of the earlier, happier days that *Colors* evokes so effectively. It is with them, with Judy Collins and the balding teaching assistants, and not in the more bumptious precincts of rock 'n' roll, that our president's heart unquestionably lies. Their happy days are here again. And Megadeth, like the rest of us, is just going to have to live with it.

I've Got Virtue:
Bill Bennett Re-moralizes
America All by Himself

June 1994

FORGIVE ME FOR BEGINNING WITH A QUOTE from Plato, the famous dead Greek: "Shall we just carelessly allow children to hear any casual tales which may be devised by casual persons, and to receive into their minds ideas for the most part the very opposite of those which we should wish them to have when they are grown up?

"We cannot. . . . Anything received into the mind at that age is likely to become indelible and unalterable; and therefore it is most important that the tales which the young first hear should be models of virtuous thought."

Is there a modern parent, shepherding his innocent tots through the media maelstrom of MTV, Sharon Stone, 2 Live Crew, and X-Men comic books, for whom these words don't carry some dark resonance?

A case in point: It is shortly after nine o'clock on a Thursday night, and like all good yuppies I am in front of the TV, watching *Seinfeld*. My three-year-old son has somehow missed his bedtime and is seated in the chair opposite, examining his toenails. My attention is consumed by the show until I realize that its plot revolves around Elaine's ability to fake orgasms. Quickly the scene shifts and the show moves to a discussion of George's inability to achieve erections. With mounting alarm I glance at my son, who is staring, wide-eyed, at the screen. George, meanwhile, is making hacking motions at his unresponsive crotch. I grab the remote and snap off the set.

"No!" my three-year-old shouts. "Let's watch Jerry! I want to see what happens to George!"

Into such scenes of parental angst lumbers now the imposing figure of William J. Bennett, carrying under his arm his enormous bestseller, *The Book of Virtues: A Treasury of Great Moral Stories*. It is a new stage in the public life of the former drug czar and secretary of education. For the moment he has shrugged off his trademark partisan belligerence. In his current incarnation he transcends politics. He aims instead to provide a moral compass to parents buffeted by the winds of societal decay, to help us rediscover the old truths, to return us to the moral roots of the West. And if he happens to be elected president along the way, well, that's fine, too.

The big book is unavoidable these days: more than a million copies in print, more than 900,000 sold. As I write, it has been nestled on the *Washington Post*'s bestseller list for eighteen weeks, on the *New York Times*'s for nineteen, and odds are that by the time you read this it will be there still. For the last eight years or so it's been axiomatic that every bestseller list, in any given week, carries at least one book by a disgruntled middle-aged white guy—Allan Bloom, Robert Bork, Tom Clancy, Rush Limbaugh, Michael Crichton, Margaret Thatcher—catapulted to success by the buying power of his fellow disgruntled middle-aged white guys. Bennett is undoubtedly, in fact famously, one of those guys, but his book breaks the mold. Reviews written even by his political enemies have been kind, if patronizing. *The Book of Virtues* is being bought, and maybe read, by liberal parents as well as conservative, by secular humanists and evangelical Protestants alike. In the magazines and newspapers it has spawned dozens of thumb-sucking op-eds and trend stories, heralding a hunger for meaning here in the nineties.

Bennett, not surprisingly, agrees. "The values thing is exploding in this country," he says. "I think we're at the edge of a major cultural seismic shift. The states are passing laws very similar to the kind that were passed in the nineteenth century, to promote morality and the development of educational and moral faculties, the development of virtue, to foster in the young an awareness of concepts like self-discipline and responsibility—what we call good character. Something's going on out there, and the book reflects that."

Surely, something *is* going on. *The Book of Virtues* is an unlikely bestseller, falling outside the usual categories of movie-star tell-alls, New Age self-help guides, and implausible financial advice that dominate the nonfiction lists. It offers instead a collection of poems, myths, fables, short stories, and philosophical extracts, very few of a vintage more recent than the 1930s. "I told my publisher I wanted to do a McGuffey Reader for the nineties," says Bennett, "and that's what I did."

The oddity is that McGuffey Readers have been out of favor with everyone but a few homeschoolers and *700 Club* viewers for more than thirty years. The fashion today is for children's books that read as if they were cobbled together in the labs of a graduate school of education. From the agitprop of the infamous *Heather Has Two Mommies* to the literal-mindedness of *Sesame Street* books, kids are treated to dumbed-down prose, limp plotting, and collections of characters whose preeminent virtue is their perfect racial and sexual balance. A moral might be permitted, on condition that it's not terribly "judgmental."

Bennett, the father of two boys (ages five and ten), has had enough of it, and to judge by the sales of his book, so have lots of parents. Most of them seem to be newly reactionary baby boomers, terrified that the libertinism of pop culture will distort their cute little Ashleys and Colins into twenty-first-century Charles Mansons, or worse, Keanu Reeveses. Like its

McGuffey prototype, *The Book of Virtues* is suffused with an austere, uncompromising moralism. The illustrations, most of them Victorian pen-and-inks, are small and spare. Each virtue gets a chapter of its own—"Self-discipline," "Courage," "Work," "Friendship," "Compassion," and so on—introduced by an erudite headnote explaining its practical application. And above each selection are a few lines that distill the moral of the story into a sound bite: "We must brace ourselves for all of life's contingencies." "Others may try to feed our ego, but it is up to us to constrain it." "Of all the vices, lust is the one many people seem to find the most difficult to control." All of these are pleasantly, even reassuringly, old-fashioned. In *The Book of Virtues*, by God, Heather has only one mommy.

Whether she will survive Mommy is another question. For children and parents lullabied by the banality of contemporary children's books, the cold-blooded resoluteness of many of Bennett's selections will come as a jolt. We meet Hilaire Belloc's "Rebecca," who enjoyed the "Furious Sport" of slamming doors. "She was not really bad at heart, but only rude and wild." Tough. She gets brained by a marble bust jogged loose by her incessant slamming. Then there's Jim, who won't mind his nanny, so a lion eats him. As punishment for assorted misdemeanors, "John, Tom, and James" grow up "ugly, and nobody cares." "The Little Girl Who Wriggles" turns into an eel and is eaten by a shark. Augustus won't eat his soup and hence starves. The parents of Godfrey Gordon Gustavus Gore, who refuses to close doors politely, threaten to send him to Singapore. We all know what they do to bad boys in Singapore.

And that's just the first fifty pages!

Some reviewers have suggested that Bennett's Victorian version of uplift—hyperjudgmentalism, you could call it—might be off-putting to tots of the Barney generation. Not so, Bennett says: "David Brooks wrote in the *Wall Street Journal* that this is a good book, etc., but one thing we won't see is kids telling their parents: 'Please, Mom and Dad, let's read the virtue book again!' Well, as a matter of fact, that's precisely what we *are* seeing. You should see my mail—parents telling me their kids are saying, 'C'mon, bring down the big book.' This book is very personal. It's the place where parents live with their children, it's the center, it's where the action is."

Bennett says he is loath to turn the book into a political instrument—"It's bigger than politics"—but he believes there is nevertheless something that politicians can learn from it.

"This book is about responsibility," he says, "this book is about character, it's about taking charge of your own life. And if there's a message official Washington needs to hear more than any other it's that this is a self-governing society, and a self-governing society requires what the Founders would call virtue. ''Tis virtue we aim at,' said John Locke. And if there's a lesson here, it's you can use that word, virtue, and not be run out of town, and may even be applauded for using it."

Even Washington couldn't breed a cynic so thoroughgoing as to believe that Bennett has exploited the "values thing" for purely political self-advancement. The book, he says, "was a labor of love," with roots in magazine pieces he did in the late 1970s, years before President Reagan selected him to head the National Endowment for the Humanities and set him up in public life.

But the book is bound up with his extremely convoluted political career nonetheless. In 1988, following his incendiary tenure as Reagan's second education secretary, which followed his incendiary tenure as head of the NEH, Bennett proved a megastar on the speakers' circuit, earning $240,000 in four months. At the same time, he signed a two-book contract with Simon & Schuster for a $187,000 advance. Before the books could get written, President Bush appointed him drug czar (officially, director of the Office of National

Drug Control Policy). Later Bush asked him to succeed Lee Atwater as chairman of the Republican National Committee. Bennett accepted. Then he unaccepted two weeks after that, when government ethics cops told him he couldn't continue his avocation as after-dinner speaker, which he needed to do, he said, because he had already spent the book advance and had to pay it back. In turning down the $125,000-a-year RNC chairmanship he made a comment that has since been engraved in the annals of Washington chutzpah: "I didn't take a vow of poverty."

The books got written. The first was a memoir called *The Devaluing of America*. The second was *The Book of Virtues*. Poverty is no longer a big worry.

The big book's explosive popularity has only added to Bennett's drawing power as a public speaker; he now gets between $20,000 and $30,000 per appearance. It has also revived a flagging public career, full of zigzags and dead ends. After he resigned as education secretary, several right-wing foundations formed a think tank, the Madison Center, with Bennett as its star. He abandoned it after four months, when Bush called him back to public office.

The drug czarship was a new job, mandated by a Congress feverish to appear to be doing something, anything, about drugs. It was also an impossible job—underfunded, with a vague portfolio and little institutional authority. Bennett quit after eighteen months. The RNC debacle was next. *Devaluing*, written hurriedly, was published to disappointing sales. At the close of the Bush administration, Bennett teamed with retiring congressman Vin Weber, HUD secretary Jack Kemp, and Jeane Kirkpatrick to form an all-star think tank called Empower America. Even here, disaster was narrowly averted. According to Republican folklore, the organization's original name was to be the Lincoln Institute for American Renewal. A perfect name: it had the Lincoln connection, "institute" lent the thing a scholarly air, and "American Renewal" had played well with focus groups during the 1992 campaign. Then someone pointed out the unfortunate acronym.

Empower America has been a disappointment, too, especially for young Republicans who considered its powerhouse lineup to be a kind of conservative equivalent of the Concert for Bangladesh. At its founding Kemp said it would be a "shadow government" to the Clinton administration; but, in the event, not quite. In 1992 Bennett was without a solid institutional grounding. Empower America provided him one. Now it needs Bennett more than he needs it. The group could fold tomorrow and Bill Bennett would still be . . . *Bill Bennett.* He has become a brand name: for some, a sage, the embodiment of the wisdom of the West, and for many others, even those less given to romanticism, a plausible candidate for president.

Bennett's support, say some Republican analysts, seems strongest not in Washington but among the party's grass roots, particularly evangelical Christians. (Those urging him to run include James Dobson, of the million-member Focus on the Family, and Gary Bauer of the traditionalist Family Research Council.) There are many ironies here. The most obvious is that Bennett is a purely Washington creature, a textbook example of the subspecies known as the anti-Washington Washingtonian.

Bennett opens *Devaluing* with an anecdote from one of his speaking engagements: "I said I could sum up my evening's remarks in a single sentence. 'Now that American values have prevailed in Eastern Europe, we should work to see to it that the same values prevail in *Washington, D.C.*' [Italics in original.] I then added, 'The American people are fine. Washington is not. The patient is in better shape than the doctor.'"

The irony is an unavoidable professional hazard for conservative activists in Washington, but for Bennett it is particularly acute, if only because the Beltway culture has been so kind to him. His professional gifts are the gifts Washington prizes most highly. He has considerable television presence, a quick mind, an ear for the sound bite, and an unerring eye for publicity. He possesses these gifts in abundance, and he has been abundantly rewarded. Before Washington discovered him—before he discovered Washington—Bennett labored in the vineyards of academe, as a professor and administrator. Now, excluding book royalties, according to a conservative estimate (by which I mean the estimate made by envious conservatives), Bennett makes $500,000 a year just for getting out of bed in the morning: $150,000 from *National Review* magazine, on whose masthead he is listed as senior editor, $150,000 from the Heritage Foundation, where he carries the title Distinguished Fellow in Cultural Policy Studies, and $200,000 from Empower America. People who remain college professors make somewhat less.

He has also availed himself of the perks that Washington lavishes on its superstars. No superstar, for example, would write his own book, and not doing so is certainly no impediment to launching a presidential campaign. Before challenging LBJ in 1964, Barry Goldwater wrote *The Conscience of a Conservative*, which was written by Brent Bozell. And John Kennedy, of course, wrote and then accepted, with well-deserved modesty, a Pulitzer for *Profiles in Courage*, which was written by Ted Sorensen.

One of the few pleasures of reading such books comes from the acknowledgments, in which, shoved up among the encomiums to wife, kids, typists, and high school track coaches, the name of the book's true author is slyly revealed. The surest clue is an excess of praise. On page 15 of *Devaluing* we read: "A very special debt of gratitude is owed to Peter Wehner. Over the years, I have come to respect and rely on him in many ways, but this was never more so than when I embarked full-time on this enterprise. . . ." Etc. And on page 16 of *Virtues* we read: "As to John Cribb, I cannot thank him enough for his efforts to make this book a reality. . . ." And so on. Getting away with this, and thinking nothing of it, is part of what it means to be a brand name.

Would the brand name retain its marketing power in the world of electoral politics? At various times Republican activists and moneymen have beseeched Bennett to run for the Senate from New York, Maryland, and North Carolina, where he lived before moving to Washington. He has declined every offer. Asked by a friend once why he refused to make the run from North Carolina, Bennett replied, "I'm afraid I might win."

"I think Bill could mount an incredibly exciting and successful campaign for president," says Bauer. "But it's not clear that he's willing to do the unexciting things you have to do to win. He's not a backslapper or a gladhander."

More dangerously, Bennett refuses to cut his rhetoric to the one-size-fits-all banality of most successful politicians. In a widely noted speech to the Heritage Foundation last December, Bennett revised his diagnosis of America's ills and Washington's relationship to them. The patient, Bennett announced, "is no longer in better shape than the doctor: When it comes to decadence, Washington has nothing on the American people."

America, said Bennett, is "a degraded society." "Specifically, our problem is what the ancients called *acedia* . . . spiritual torpor, an absence of zeal for divine things. . . . Acedia arises from a heart steeped in the worldly and carnal, and from a low esteem of divine things." The consequence is "a coarseness, a cynicism, a banality, and a vulgarity."

You don't have to be a Republican to wonder how this would play at a full-dress political rally, after a warm-up of marching bands and pom-pom girls. The Heritage speech showed a far darker Bennett than the one reflected in his books. "Conservatives need to be wary of fretfulness," says

the Bennett of *The Devaluing of America.* "Americans don't
want to be led by people who are sour, cynical, negative, or
hopelessly pessimistic. . . . Conservatives should lighten up,
enjoy life, and show it. . . . It is better to light a candle than
curse the darkness."

With *The Book of Virtues* Bennett lit a candle that may
in time become a bonfire, providing comfort to millions of
nervous parents trying to indemnify their children against
Seinfeld and worse (Madonna). It's a large achievement that,
as he says, could be diminished by the crudities of politics.

That's a risk he may be willing to take anyway. His famous
ambivalence about running for office remains—even now,
when the office is the presidency.

"I don't know," he says. "I'm going to think about it this
summer—think about it hard. You know, if I'd listened to all
those people who wanted me to run for the Senate, I never
would have done this book. This book wouldn't exist. So . . ."
His voice trails off.

"You know, you've just got to trust your instincts. I've
trusted my instincts this far, and everything's turned out pretty
well."

The Donald
Writes a Book

September 1990

WHEN THE BOOKS EDITOR OF THE *WALL STREET*
Journal phoned me, I told my girl to put the call right through.
The *Journal* is a truly world-class institution for which I have
enormous respect. Besides, the newspaper business, in which
the *Journal* team is a major player, is an industry with which
I've always been fascinated. I'm not saying I was panting.
People who make deals do not pant. But I was willing to talk.

"Andrew," this editor said to me, "you *must* review that
Trump book." Frankly, I was not surprised to hear from her.
She happens to be one of the top editors in her chosen field
and a major, major talent. We had done numerous deals over
the past two years, and, to be honest, I think even my critics will admit that we both benefited in a maximized way
from those deals. My work filled the upper righthand corner of this page, which I happen to know is a very sensitive
matter with this particular editor, and I walked away with
more than a few dollars in my pocket, which I was very
happy to have.

So to myself I'm thinking: This could be class. This could
be a go. I would not be truly unhappy to possess this book,
although I knew that the smirking cover photo might keep
my wife, who is terrific, awake nights. To be in a reviewing
situation with this man's book could be a fantastic opportu-

nity. But I had doubts of which I had to unburden myself. That's who I am. That's me.

"Look," I said to this editor, who is brilliant and back with whom I go way, "there's one problem. The book stinks. It is a menace. Spend twenty-five minutes with it, and you find yourself thinking and talking exactly the way this man thinks and talks: self-congratulatory, dissembling, superficial, and periphrastic, which is a word I happen to know of which the Donald has never heard. I will not take the risk of sounding like a buffoon for the rest of my life. I cannot review this book."

"I'll pay you extra," she said.

The book arrived the next day, and my modesty will not be offended if I admit to you that I was right on target: *Surviving at the Top* is the thinnest, least interesting celebrity book since the publication of the eighteenth rewrite of Bob Hope's memoirs, which is nothing against Bob, who is a dear friend and very old.

Like innumerable Americans, literally, I had been gagging for months reading about Donald's incredibly sleazy personal problems and then had recoiled at the transparently phony denials of his massive business failures. You would think that we, as a nation, would have had enough of a man who induced a coast-to-coast upchuck for the better part of a year. But you would be wrong. *Surviving at the Top* has attained an incredibly high position on some of the most widely respected bestseller lists in this country. Who, you ask me, is buying this book in such fabulous numbers?

First are the people who are in an obsessive relationship with the Donald's personal situation. They are, as he puts it, the scum of the earth, which in all fairness they have every right to be. Unfortunately, *Surviving at the Top* is totally lacking in personal information of the tabloid variety; if it's gossip you want, I respectfully suggest that you try Liz Smith, a true pro of whom I am most fond. Ivana is one very special lady—brains *and* body, the Donald admits. But here's the bottom line on this class act whom he was proud to call wife before she started monthly skin peels: "We seem to be headed in different directions."

Donald, you're saying, we *knew* that. You're saying: Fine, okay, then how about Marla? A "terrific person," Donald writes, "but my relationship with her was not the cause of the trouble between Ivana and me." *That's it.* Now, Marla is not a nothing lady. This is a lady who has worked in film; this is a lady who on numerous occasions has expressed deep concern about our environment; this is a lady who, in a famous TV interview, achieved the unimaginable feat of making Diane Sawyer appear intelligent by comparison. But of all this the Donald says nothing!

Let us just say that this is a very savvy gentleman, a guy who plays his cards incredibly close to the vest. This is also a guy who has happened to achieve at a very high strata a kind of success that is fabulous. That's why most of his book is aimed at the readers who are stupid—although I respect them totally as people. These are people whose hunger for business books is insatiable. They are convinced that *Surviving at the Top* will unlock the secrets of success, Trump-style—that it will explain how a man can botch his deals to the point where his debts exceed his assets by one-third of a billion dollars and still write a book called *Surviving at the Top*.

The answer is simple. First, convince scores of terrific bankers from some of the hugest banks in the world to lend you very substantial sums of financing. These sums allow you to spend megalomaniacally, which helps you convince other brilliantly creative bankers to act in an accommodating mode when it comes time to pay off the first terrific bankers.

Do either the Donald or I have to draw you pictures to explain that those terrific people will therefore do everything in their power to keep you from going down that chute? Suddenly you will find that these are some fabulously patient lenders with whom you are privileged to be doing business.

It will be tough. It will be a challenge. But in the final analysis it will be a deal.

Bill Moyers and
the Power of Myth

August 1991

BARRY GOLDWATER SAYS OF BILL MOYERS, "Every time I see him, I get sick to my stomach and want to throw up." But the former senator is, yet again, either before or behind his times. Bill Moyers's standing as the conscience of America is one of the stipulated facts of our national life. *Texas Monthly* says he is "the standard bearer of the best we see in ourselves." Jennifer Lawson, programming chief of PBS, says he is a "national treasure." Jackie Onassis calls him one of her heroes. Barbara Jordan takes it a step further: "I'd like to see him as president."

She is not alone. This spring and summer the word rippled through Democratic circles that Moyers was willing to make Jordan's dream a reality. The rumor gained circulation in a column by the *New York Times*'s Leslie Gelb on July 3: "He was not surprised when I asked him whether he should be thinking about running for president. 'I would. It would be fun,' Bill Moyers said in his intense, soft-spoken way. But for the next two years, no, he has obligations." Moyers told me the same thing in a recent interview.

Articles suggesting a Moyers candidacy first surfaced in the mid-1970s, not long after his public-television basting of the Nixon administration during the Watergate scandal. His demurrals were apparently sincere, but he flashed just enough thigh to inspire further attempts to recruit him for high office, including propositions from Jimmy Carter to become director of the CIA, secretary of education, and finally Carter's chief of staff. In 1988 a troupe of Democrats renewed the entreaties, and when they failed, Paul Simon urged drafting him for vice president.

A Moyers candidacy is not as implausible as you might think. He is the pure outsider candidate. The image he has created over the years is of a sojourner, unsullied by commerce, unstinting in his quest for the straight dope, steadfast in his dedication to a country that, in his phrase, "refuses to face the truth about itself." But he also has plenty of inside experience. As deputy director of the Peace Corps under John Kennedy and then as LBJ's closest aide from 1964 to 1967, he is credited as one of the architects of the Great Society. In the aftermath of the Gulf War, when Democratic congressmen gathered in Virginia for their annual "issues conference," they called upon Moyers to deliver the keynote address.

Moyers's speech proved medicinal—laden with the lofty phrases familiar to TV audiences. He spoke of "an ethic of cooperation," "the soul of America," "the party of the wounded," and "the conversation of democracy." "A renewal of community" followed "a new political compact," and so on. The congressmen especially appreciated Moyers's congratulating them—he surely was the first to do so—on their votes against the war in the Gulf.

The speech was notable for its curious play of pronouns. Throughout he referred to "you Democrats" and "your party." He even said, "I left partisanship behind when I left the White House in 1967 for journalism." But no one there seriously questioned Moyers's Democratic loyalty, which is intense and unremitting. But then, almost nobody does, because the subject never comes up. For this Moyers relies on a docile press and a gift for avoiding the stickier questions raised by a long and various career.

Except for turning aside suitors, Moyers's involvement in recent campaigns has been limited to his appearances on PBS. Lately he has been struck by the debilitating effect of negative campaign ads on "the conversation of democracy" around "the national campfire." He first addressed it in a show called *The 30-Second President*, which featured an interview with Tony Schwartz, creator of the anti-Goldwater "Daisy" commercial in 1964. The black-and-white footage, you'll remember, starred a little girl picking daisy petals until a nuclear explosion caught her attention for the last time. The commercial was progenitor to the negative campaign spots that Moyers believes have "trivialized" the conversation of democracy.

Moyers's real achievement in the broadcast, however, was to dwell on the commercial while disguising his own role in creating it. "I was in the thick" of the 1964 campaign, he admits, a "young fellow up from Texas" working in the White House. (Moyers had been working in Washington for four years by the time of the campaign.) One of his jobs, he tells us, was to act as "liaison" between the White House and the admen. A liaison, of course, is someone caught in the middle. In case we didn't get the point, Moyers says of Schwartz: "I never met him, by the way, until a year ago." Like the critics who praised the show so lavishly, Moyers neglects to mention (although other veterans of the '64 campaign are more than happy to) that it was he who insisted that the admen raise the nuclear issue against Goldwater and that indeed it was he who commissioned and approved the "attack" ads, including the Daisy spot. At hour's end Moyers delivers the Olympian summing up, in which he confesses to an uncharacteristic ambivalence: "We have to look for alternatives—using TV but using it wisely."

This sly prevarication runs through some of Moyers's other work as well. He has, for example, used Republican scandals as occasions for sermons about betrayals of trust, government

run amok, even as his own involvement in one of the seamier
episodes of government malfeasance slips quietly down the
memory hole. Johnson once called Moyers "my vice president
in charge of everything." By all accounts the tag was accurate. According to classified documents unearthed by the
Church Committee on intelligence abuses in 1976, and others
obtained by David Garrow for his *The FBI and Martin Luther
King* (1981), while at the White House Moyers tracked the
bureau's infamous campaign against King. The surveillance,
begun under Kennedy, was broadened under Johnson. The
rationale at the time, and the one Moyers clings to on the few
occasions he has discussed his involvement, was that King's
association with supposed Communists endangered the civil
rights movement.

As the campaign against King progressed, FBI Director
J. Edgar Hoover routinely forwarded to the White House summaries of the King wiretaps, which were placed not only in
King's home and office but also in his hotel rooms around
the country. The summaries covered not only King's dealings
with associates but also his sexual activities. After receiving
one such summary, Moyers instructed the FBI to disseminate
it widely throughout the executive branch, to Dean Rusk,
Robert McNamara, Carl Rowan, and many others. Moyers
was also aware at the time of Hoover's efforts to leak the King
material to the press.

Moyers's interest in King was not limited to the "Communist" scare. King was allied with a group even more worri-
some to the Johnson White House: dissident Democrats. At
the Democratic convention in Atlantic City in 1964, King
assisted civil rights associates in a credential challenge to the
all-white Mississippi delegation. The White House, fearing
trouble for the fall campaign, instructed the FBI to intensify
surveillance of the dissenters during the convention. As a
result a wiretap was installed in King's Atlantic City hotel

room. One bureau memo reported happily, "We have been able to keep the White House and others very currently informed concerning King and these important matters." The agent in charge of the bugging, Cartha "Deke" DeLoach, kept in telephone contact with Moyers and his fellow Johnson aide, Walter Jenkins, throughout the convention, and the two aides successfully countered the King group's maneuvers, allowing the good old boys to take their seats on the convention floor.

Moyers later wrote a note thanking DeLoach for his help. DeLoach replied: "Thank you for your very thoughtful and generous note concerning our operation in Atlantic City. . . . I'm certainly glad that we were able to come through with vital tidbits from time to time which were of assistance to you and Walter. You know you have only to call on us when a similar situation arises."

It soon did. Not long before the election, Jenkins was arrested in a bathroom stall at the YMCA on a charge of "disorderly conduct." Johnson, convinced that Jenkins was somehow set up by Goldwater's campaign operatives, ordered Moyers to gather information on the sexual histories of Goldwater's staff. Moyers called DeLoach, who reported back that he had been unable to find anything of political use. Ten years later Moyers won an Emmy for two PBS shows on Watergate, both noteworthy for his fiery indignation over Richard Nixon's abuse of government power for political ends. The outrage was displayed again in the two ninety-minute PBS shows he produced on the Iran-Contra affair.

Of his experience in the White House, Moyers says, "I've never exonerated the past. But I've never let myself be imprisoned by the past, either. I worked in Washington in those years, but I'm not a journalist practicing in those years—I'm a journalist now. I can't let myself as a journalist be stayed by the indiscretions of those years, any more than [former

Nixon aide] Bill Safire can." The difference, of course, is that
when Safire worked in the White House, he was, as it were,
the buggee.

These days Moyers is increasingly distracted from the affairs
of state by the lure of spiritualism and pop psychology. Moyers's
greatest discovery in this area was Joseph Campbell, a professor at Sarah Lawrence and a veteran of the New Age circuit
of self-realization workshops. Among Campbell's groupies was
the movie producer George Lucas, and it was on Lucas's California ranch that Moyers and Campbell filmed much of the
six-hour-long special *The Power of Myth with Bill Moyers*.
   The show was a stunning success by the fragile standards
of PBS. Total viewership, according to PBS, topped thirty
million. The series' companion volume was on the bestseller
lists for seventy-four weeks. Throughout the show, Campbell
discourses on the great spiritual traditions, and many lesser
ones too. Borrowing from Jung the notion of archetypes,
Campbell argued that all religious myths were at bottom the
same story of the quest for self-transcendence. Odysseus,
Jesus, the Bodhidharma, Moses, the young aborigine on a
walkabout: all, according to Campbell, were doing essentially
the same thing. Campbell's "teaching" shares an additional
benefit with other forms of pop monism. Ethics are, as he puts
it, "out of date." Moyers has pointed out that for Campbell
the one "unpardonable sin" was "not being alert," a quasi-
religious message at once risk-free and undemanding, and
so vague as to fit almost anywhere:

> CAMPBELL: To see through the fragments of time to the full
> power of original being—that is the function of art.
> MOYERS: Beauty is an expression of that rapture of being
> alive.
> CAMPBELL: Every moment should be such an experience.

MOYERS: And what we are going to become tomorrow is not important as compared to this experience.
CAMPBELL: This is the great moment, Bill.

Campbell is also a historian. Here is his account of America's founding: "When you add one and seven and seven and six, you get twenty-one, which is the age of reason, is it not? It was in 1776 that the thirteen states declared independence. Thirteen is the number of getting out of the field of the bounds of twelve into the transcendent. . . . These men were very conscious of the number thirteen as the number of resurrection and rebirth and new life, and they played it up."

Undeterred by Campbell's death in 1987, Moyers has continued his public quest in more recent shows about the "men's movement" and other offspring of Campbell's work. In particular Moyers has featured Sam Keen, another academic turned workshop maestro, and Robert Bly, a plump poet from Minnesota who serenades men's seminars with an untuned lyre. In these shows—*A Gathering of Men, Your Mythic Journey, Where the Soul Lives*—Moyers's camera lingers on the pale men and women who crowd the workshops, sitting cross-legged and shoeless on the floor. Most complain of a profound inarticulateness, an inability to express their feelings, but they do so with startling volubility. Catch phrases recur—"rage," "grief," "the male mother," "the warrior within," "the hairy man"—without much indication as to what they might mean. "Rage," Bly says, is "rooted in the industrial revolution" and is "a door between male and female." Ah yes.

This descent into pop spiritualism is particularly unfortunate given the quality of some of Moyers's earlier work. A few shows from the mid-1980s—a memoir of his hometown, *Marshall, Texas; Marshall, Texas,* and his study of urban pathologies, *The Vanishing Family,* for example—display a gift for observation beyond the reach of all but the finest documentarians. Moyers insists his more recent broadcasts merely continue his reportorial calling. "That's just one of the beats I cover as a journalist," he told me. "I'm aware that the life of the spirit and the quest for self-transformation is a big story, and the press is ignoring it." But he brings to the subject none of the skepticism he applied, say, to the rise of evangelical Christianity, a much more widespread movement he basted in several shows in the late seventies and eighties. The comparison with Moyers's leaning toward Campbell and asking, "How do I slay the dragon within me?" is depressingly acute.

The kicker is that all this indulgence is made possible through a generous grant from the public. Moyers rejoined public broadcasting in 1986 after leaving CBS News, where he had earned $20,000 a week. He quit, he said, because "if you're going to have impact in this medium, you need regularity and frequency." CBS could provide neither. Since forming his own production company, Public Affairs Television, Inc., in 1986, Moyers has produced 136 hours of television.

As an institution, public television carries the nimbus of self-sacrifice; it appears as a sweatshop of altruistic craftsmen laboring *pro bono publico*. And indeed the salaries of public TV employees are capped, like those of other civil servants. Independent producers, however, face no such constraints. How much money Moyers has made as a private businessman by availing himself of public broadcasting is a mystery. The flow of funds within the hermetic world of public TV is one of its tightest secrets. (Though government-funded, the Corporation for Public Broadcasting is exempt from the Freedom of Information Act.) Moyers himself says only, "I've been lucky. I've always made a nice living."

Moyers draws the bulk of his funding from two sources: mostly left-leaning tax-exempt foundations and corporate sponsors. Since tax-exempt foundations are forbidden by law from supporting for-profit enterprises, the money is given to a middleman—in Moyers's case, usually WNET "in support of" particular programming. The middleman then contracts with the production company to produce the shows. (For Moyers, the costs apparently include not only his own salary but that of his wife, Judith, who is president of PAT and is usually listed as "executive producer" or "series consultant" on his shows, and on at least one show, that of his son Cope, "researcher.") In other businesses this circuitous routing of funds would be called money-laundering. Within the cloisters of PBS, it's business as usual—and, of course, perfectly legal.

The amounts donated are considerable. In 1989, for example, WNET received $2.5 million from the MacArthur Foundation and $850,000 from the Charles Stewart Mott Foundation for Moyers's television shows, according to IRS records. CPB kicked in another $1.25 million the same year. In 1988, IRS records show, PAT was authorized to receive another $3 million from the Florence and John Schumann Foundation in New Jersey, which annually doles out about $3.5 million. At the time of that grant, the Schumann Foundation was headed by William Mullins, an old friend of Moyers's from Peace Corps days. When Mullins died in 1990, the foundation named a new president—Bill Moyers. The same year, it awarded an extra $300,000 to Moyers's landlord, WNET, "towards production costs of the series, 'Environment: Your Own Backyard.'" The WNET grant was the second largest the foundation awarded that year, almost 10 percent of the total handed out.

Moyers's way with corporations is equally impressive. "We can leverage the funds very well," he told me. "You get a dollar from MacArthur, say, and you go to a corporation for a matching grant. You get another dollar there, and then you go to public television and ask for money based on that. I've raised four dollars for every one I've raised from public television." Paine Webber, Chevron, Weyerhaeuser, General

Motors, and Johnson and Johnson are among those corporations that have donated large sums to PAT, although each refuses to release even general figures. This year's corporate sponsor is the insurance company Mutual of America, which likewise declines to say how large its grant was.

Television tie-ins—books and tapes adapted from broadcast shows—can bring in still more money, and here too Moyers has been a leader. The practice of profiting from these "after-sales" is controversial even within the public broadcasting establishment. One independent producer critical of "tie-ins," Larry Adelman, has written that "the program itself [becomes] an ideal commercial for the cassette (and book, record, and other program tie-ins). And unlike thirty-second [commercials], it's guaranteed to be watched ('previewed') by those already interested in the product." Moyers demurs: "There's some money in those sales. Not a lot."

As the Los Angeles–based watchdog group COMINT has documented, the Campbell series has sold a whopping 200,000 cassettes through PBS Video, which pays a royalty of at least 30 percent (Moyers splits royalties with two coproducers). *A Gathering of Men* has sold at least 48,000 units, at a price of $39.95. The cheaper *Amazing Grace*, another Moyers show, has sold 48,000. The books also do well. Seven Locks Press sold more than 40,000 copies of a spin-off from *The Secret Government*, one of Moyers's Iran-contra shows, with Moyers again sharing royalties with his coproducer. More than 750,000 copies of *The Power of Myth* are in print, and *The World of Ideas* inspired a spin-off book that also made the bestseller lists after being plugged on the shows. PAT's catalogue of shows has by now acquired a hefty market value. How much it is worth won't be known unless Moyers sells it, as he might if he finds another line of work, like running for president.

The odds that Moyers will contradict his public line and run for the White House next year are very long. He told me, however, that next year will be the last in which he makes a "major commitment" to public TV. "It will be my twentieth year in the business. I plan to quietly stand back after that." Or maybe not so quietly. Bill Moyers's America, after all, is a country that desperately needs Bill Moyers—a theme to which his program titles, notwithstanding their various subject matter, attest: *Moyers: The Public Mind, Moyers: God and Politics, Moyers: Project Censored, Moyers: In Search of the Constitution, Moyers: Sports for Sale.*

The truest model for a Moyers candidacy is perhaps that of Pat Robertson. Like the Reverend Robertson, Moyers has left behind a seamy past to take to the airwaves, where he tells tall tales to the gullible, appropriating their confusions, only to administer a salve of undemanding reassurance. And like Robertson, Moyers has made a nice living doing so, masterfully employing all the techniques of the video age. The politics of both are resolute, moralistic, and unyielding.

The differences too are telling: whereas Robertson draws his budget from the voluntary donations of dupes, Moyers taps the public trough, through tax-free foundations and tax-write-off corporate donations, and a government-subsidized network whose devotion to him is boundless. And whereas Robertson's religion relies on a historical tradition and common text against which it can be measured and criticized, the spiritualism that Moyers has lately been retailing comprehends only the unfalsifiable whims of pop shrinks, infinitely elastic and malleable. Neither, it's safe to say, is a credible guide for politics, or life. To the apolitical among us Bill Moyers is an Elmer Gantry of the New Age. To the Democrats, he is a Henry Wallace for the 1990s.

Bob McNamara's Brand

June 1995

I'M A LITTLE BIT WORRIED. AS I WRITE THIS, in early June, it's been a full month since I've read a nationally published article trashing Robert McNamara. All spring, immediately preceding the publication of McNamara's memoirs and then for a luscious period thereafter, you couldn't pick up a magazine or a reputable newspaper without exposing yourself to a shower of bile, all of it directed at our diminutive and bespectacled former secretary of defense. *National Review* and the *American Spectator* pitched in, of course, but so did the *New York Times* and the *Boston Globe*, and *Time* and *Newsweek*, and the *New Yorker* and the *New Republic*— even the *Nation*! For a while there, many of us McNamara-despisers thought we'd died and gone to heaven (a fate, incidentally, that McNamara himself is unlikely to enjoy).

And then—silence. What gives? Apparently the scribes have moved on; never has the press's short attention span been so criminally obvious. I feel like a guy at a college beer bust who senses the buzz just starting to kick in and wants to *part-ay down*, only to discover that everybody has gone off to the library to cram for a chem final. But for all that, I am an optimist; I am one of those who believe the keg is half full rather than half empty. And speaking only for myself, I'm ready for another draft.

My interest in McNamara is intensified because he exemplifies a peculiar Washington phenomenon. In Washington people fail up. The city is exempt from the laws of professional gravity. No other city is so accommodating of failure, so friendly to the people who fail. Large awards await the bunglers and bobblers, the has-beens and wannabees-who-never-could. Our present mayor, to cite an obvious example, destroyed the city's finances, smoked crack on TV, went to prison—and then got reelected. Other failures have shown even greater artfulness. You can see them cruising K Street in chauffeured Town Cars, cashing large checks for their "consulting" businesses, digging into filets at the Palm. Here's the Iran-Contra bungler, awarded a popular radio show for his work destroying the Reagan administration. Over there is the manager of the 1992 Bush campaign, mulling offers from candidates to work his magic again in 1996. And over here is the chief strategist for Jimmy Carter during the Iranian hostage crisis—why, he's the secretary of state!

McNamara is spiritual father to them all. He is the architect of a career breathtaking in the scope of its screwups, a clockwork progression of failure and reward, error and advancement. Imagine a friend who comes to visit. The first night he cooks you dinner and sets fire to the kitchen. The next morning he accidentally electrocutes the cat. He blows his nose in the curtains and never flushes the toilet. He borrows your car and drives through the garage door, then spreads a rare infection to your kids. By the third day you make the decision: *You ask him to move in with you.*

This is the pattern of McNamara's career. At Ford Motors, in the late 1950s, he designed the sclerotic top-down management system that almost sank the American automobile industry; for good measure, he oversaw the production of the Edsel. Accordingly, JFK handed him the Pentagon. There McNamara got the idea for the Vietnam War—the Edsel of American foreign policy. So awed was the Washington establishment that it placed him at the head of the World Bank, in hopes that he might do for the international economy what he had done for the American military. And he did! Within ten years he had doubled the amount of money loaned, and lost, to third world kleptocracies like Brazil and the Central African Empire. He was Midas in reverse. Wherever he draped his hand, industries wilted, economies collapsed, corpses piled up.

No one should have been surprised, then, that when McNamara chose to write the story of his life, it should have turned out to be a disaster by every literary measure: mendacious, sentimental, shameless in its exculpation, oily in its tone, a book so badly written that no one would ever really want to buy it. And of course it has been a rousing bestseller.

How does one explain a life thus charmed? His good looks? They may indeed have dazzled back in the days when no one minded goofy wire rims and the stink of Brylcreem. His sensitivity? It's true he cried often, and still does—the one time I met him, at a think-tank luncheon, he teared up over the Cuban Missile Crisis—and in the pre–Alan Alda sixties a man's capacity to cry could still disarm unwary companions. But none of this is sufficient. Washington's inverted culture, where failure propels a man ever upward, bespeaks a kind of masochism. Of course, the actual pain is dispersed to the country at large. But for the professional failure Washington remains safe harbor. Within weeks of the publication of the book, McNamara had been called "evil," a "liar," and a "hypocrite." Out in the heartland, a few Vietnam vets even sued him. Here in Washington, Katharine Graham threw him a book party. Everybody who's anybody was there.

Bad Girls Don't Cry

May 1994

WHITHER MADONNA? "APRIL WAS A BAD MONTH for Madonna," said the *Washington Post* Style section, as the cruelest month drew to a close. "She used to be shocking. Now she's just low-class."

Meee-*ow!* The Style section's judgment carries considerable weight—as an arbiter of *les affaires show biz* it ranks just below the *Los Angeles Times*'s Calendar section and, of course, *People*. So when Style takes a feline swipe at, let's face it, one of the most boffo stars in the history of the universe, attention must be paid.

Anti-Madonna sentiment is everywhere, seeping through the popular culture like a contagion. A new book, *The I Hate Madonna Handbook*, has just hit the stores, compiled by a woman who identifies herself as "a former fan." Just as telling, Madonna was the subject of a revisionist *étude* in *Entertainment Weekly*, by that magazine's most scholarly critic-at-large. It was a devastating blow for a woman whom the magazine once regularly referred to as a "pop icon."

"Shockingly passé," said the headline. "Her once-exhilarating bravado and impudence have curdled into a sullen, crude rebelliousness," wrote Ken Tucker. "As a feminist culture hero, she can't muster a critique of sexism as cogent as the ones offered by the women in bands like the

Breeders and Bikini Kill." Her rebelliousness—crude! Her critiques—uncogent! Bikini Kill musters better than Madonna! One can imagine the poor woman reading these hurtful words and raising dewy eyes to the handlers and sycophants who still surround her. "What's 'cogent' mean?" she would ask, but the pain would be too deep for words. Madonna has a right to be hurt—puzzled, too. The proximate cause of her curdling seems to be a recent appearance with David Letterman. She gave Letterman a pair of panties on the air; she used the f-word fourteen times, according to *People*'s accountants; she bragged of urinating in the shower; she refused to leave when her time was up. Within days she was struggling vainly to recoup. She said her cursing, for example, "was a protest against censorship." Earlier she would have been honored for her gutsy resistance to Victorian repression. Earlier, in other words, Ken Tucker would have bought it. No longer. Times have turned against her.

To understand how odd this turning is, you must review Madonna's career. Her music videos were considered pathbreaking because they showed her (as the quaint phrase went) in various stages of undress, crawling between the legs of men in sado-masochistic poses. Her documentary, *Truth or Dare*, was widely hailed for the moment when she exposed her breasts. Her book, *Sex*, consisting almost entirely of pictures of herself nude, sold 50,000 copies in a couple of days, at $50 a pop. In published interviews she discussed her favorite types of oral sex. She simulated—at least we all hoped it was simulated—masturbation during her stage shows.

And for doing so she saw her career thrive in the pages of Style and *Entertainment Weekly* and elsewhere. Now, mysteriously, she has gone too far. She must feel like Babe Ruth, who during a ballgame once ate a dozen hot dogs, four boxes of Cracker Jack, six pickles, and two cones of cotton candy, washed down with half a dozen beers. Before taking the field in the seventh inning he topped it off with an apple, and promptly passed out. When he came to, he said, "I guess I shouldn't have eaten that apple."

"The revolution is like Saturn," wrote the poet Büchner about the death of Danton. "It eats its children." And smacks its lips, too. The Robespierres of the revolution that has transformed our pop culture over the last generation are a pitiless lot—and disingenuous, to boot. Only Style and its fellow arbiters seem to know when the appropriately "shocking" (masturbating on stage) descends into the inappropriately "low-class" (saying "fuck" on late-night TV). Madonna's real crime, I suspect, was longevity. She has been boffo for almost a decade, after all. The revolution craves novelty; it is rooted in the short attention span. And because its craving never slackens, it must create new icons and dismantle old ones with amazing speed. Madonna's decade of success is like a century when measured in the dog years of pop fame.

So icons come, icons go. And then, sometimes, they come again. Depending on how things turn out, we grow to miss them, in time grant them a reprieve, even—if their replacements prove unappealing—beckon them to reclaim their former stature. Though it seems impossible today, there was a brief moment when Elvis was eclipsed by Bobby Darin, and Marilyn Monroe by Mamie Van Doren. Before long Elvis and MM returned in triumph, when their fans outgrew their own capriciousness. The same happy fate may await Madonna. Again I quote Style, from another article several months ago: "Hillary Clinton has replaced Madonna as our leading cult figure." This is very bad news for Mrs. Clinton. It is very good news for Madonna, who even now must be plotting to unseat this pretender to the throne, this Mamie Van Doren of the nineties.

Public
Places

A Sea of Stars

November 1989

THE DANCER AND ACTOR GREGORY HINES WAS
telling me there were so many homeless people in his Manhattan neighborhood that he felt compelled to come to Washington for the next day's "Housing Now!" march on the mall.
As I scribbled dutifully in my reporter's notebook, an elderly
woman tapped Hines on the shoulder. "Are you Dick Gregory?" she asked.

Thus the problem: The Left is suffering from a surfeit of
celebrities, and as a consequence the currency of stardom itself has been devalued. The elderly woman had never heard
of Gregory Hines, and, since she had paid $150 to come to
this "Housing Now!" cocktail party in a Capitol Hill hotel
on the promise of meeting stars (250 of them, according to
the press releases), her disappointment was palpable. "Where
are they?" she asked, with a slight stomp of her foot, after
Hines had moved on. As if in answer, a tall, handsome man
approached and gestured to my notebook.

"It's good to see so many people turn out for a good
cause," he said. I understood at once that he was a celebrity
and that he meant to be interviewed. I obliged, though I
hadn't the slightest idea who he was. "In my consciousness,
the homeless are everywhere," he said.

"What have you been in?" the woman demanded suddenly.
Taken aback, the fellow held up two fingers. "You might

have seen me in *V?*" he said. The woman frowned. His voice rose hopefully: "*Beastmaster?*" *Nada.* "I'm developing a project with Fonda right now," he continued, turning back to me. "Been doing a lot of writing." He introduced us to his wife, who looked a lot like Connie Chung but wasn't. The elderly woman lumbered away.

As the party progressed, one of the "Housing Now!" flacks confided, with a note of panic in her voice: "Many of my best celebs are still in the air!" A chartered plane from Los Angeles—which the flack pledged was crammed with "one of the most fabulous outpourings from the celebrity community I've ever seen"—was three hours late getting into Dulles airport. Meanwhile, the $150 customers made do with the huge buffets set around ice sculpture, several bars manned by free-pouring bartenders, a passable band, and Gregory Hines. I noticed the fellow from *V* disconsolately talking to his wife in the corner.

The "celebrity community" the flack referred to is the network of left-wing performers who can be counted on to spare a weekend for a demonstration on behalf of the homeless, the FMLN, the ozone layer, abortion rights—whatever's on that week's menu. In the early eighties the network was notoriously vast, and organizers could afford to be selective: Sometimes it seemed as if nothing less than a Streep would do. But over the last few years, response from the community has fallen off, and the organizers have apparently had to rely on whoever has nothing else to do. Increasingly, at celebrity fundraisers, the question buzzing through the press corps is: "Who's that?" And the answer is likely to be, as a photographer told me at the "Housing Now!" party: "I think that's the guy who was on those episodes of *Wiseguy* where Vinnie was assigned to assassinate the guy but he fell in love with the blonde chick who was his sister. But I'm not sure." Try fitting that in a photo caption for the Style section.

* * *

At last the star-laden bus from Dulles arrived. I stood in the hotel vestibule outside the party, watching celebrities make their way through the crush of security and cameramen and onlookers. Time and again, the TV lights from *Entertainment Tonight*'s crew would switch on, bodies would jostle, cameras would whir; I would crane my neck, expecting, I guess, Paul Newman, and there . . . there would be a rather menacing-looking fellow who, for all I could tell, was a hotel dishwasher masquerading in leather.

To be fair, I should add that it's still relatively easy to spot a celebrity, even if you don't know precisely who he is. There's the leather outfit, first and foremost. All the men have jaws like granitic outcroppings, aquiline noses, and long hair moussed and brushed straight back to reveal hugely exaggerated widow's peaks. The famous women, for their part, share a preference for tights, homburgs pressed down in the manner of Ben Turpin, and furiously batting eyes. Anorexia seems still to be a problem. They are tanned and programmed to talk self-effacingly. But the question was never far beneath the surface: "Who's that?"

In one of his standard stump speeches, Jesse Jackson says, "We can't all be famous, because we can't all be well known." He should pass the word the next time he's in L.A. Beyond that, however, you wouldn't be overreaching to find in the tepid celebrity turnout a metaphor for the march itself. That "Housing Now!" was a bust is acknowledged by all but the cheeriest do-gooders. Before the march, sponsors were wisely tight-lipped with projections of the turnout, but informal talk of "hundreds of thousands" wasn't uncommon. The official Park District count was about forty thousand.

I managed to rouse myself for the celebrity breakfast the next morning, when the Hollywood contingent walked from their hotel to a nearby shelter to break bread with some real homeless folks, for whom, after all, they had given Hollywood's last full measure of devotion—a coach seat on a chartered jet and a shot to be on *Entertainment Tonight.* Reverend Jackson showed up—of course—and he created a stir, but for the most part the celebrities went unnoticed. I did see at least one person I recognized, though. He was tall, goodlooking. He was talking to one of the homeless. He leaned down, the better to be heard. *"Beastmaster?"* he shouted, hopefully, but the homeless fellow just shook his head.

Choice Cuts

June 1989

IT HAS BECOME VIRTUALLY IMPOSSIBLE THESE days to make a Hollywood starlet shut up. Sincere, honorable persons of good faith, who believe with every fiber of their being that Hollywood actresses should be summarily removed from public discourse, have seen the right to silence bimbos steadily eroded by activist courts careening under the influence of the liberal media. There is, most prominently, what we might call the First Amendment Problem. In the early sixties, the now notorious Warren Court discovered, through typically tortuous reasoning, an "excretion from the penumbra" of the Constitution's free speech clause allowing the court to extend the right of unfettered expression of ideas even to people who have never had an idea: even, in other words, to overpaid, heavily mascara'd blondes who perform on television in nightgowns. Almost immediately after the ruling was handed down, Jayne Mansfield endorsed George Murphy in his bid for a Senate seat, and Mamie Van Doren started bitching about Quemoy and Matsu. Frank introduced Marilyn to JFK. From there, argue the starlets' opponents, it was but a short slide down the slippery slope to Hanoi Jane.

Now we have the Hollywood Women's Political Committee. Since its founding in 1984, the committee has slowly insinuated itself into the life of Washington. It obtrudes at that point in the cultural matrix where the interests of show business and politics most conspicuously intersect: celebrity and money. Wherever leggy TV stars slink and sashay—at a cocktail party in a Beverly Hills bistro or at a rubber-chicken dinner in the ballroom of a Washington hotel—there's bound to be money, which means that, sooner or later, politicians will show up too. The committee's first function was a Mondale-Ferraro campaign dinner in August 1984, which hauled in $1 million. In 1986, during three humid hours around Barbra Streisand's swimming pool, it raised $1.5 million for Democratic Senate candidates. More recently, the HWPC has taken to bestowing the Barbara Jordan Award for Political Courage and Commitment; the first (and so far only) winner was . . . Barbara Jordan. The event raised $150,000.

Despite its potential as a political juggernaut, the HWPC likes to pace itself, selecting only a few "issues" a year upon which to concentrate—an understandable caution, since starlets, no matter how many balls are in the air, can seldom juggle more than one at a time (unless they're a producer's). This year the group's three issues, according to Marge Tabankin, executive director of the HWPC, are a "non-interventionist foreign policy," the environment, and "choice." This last is the current euphemism for legalized abortion, a truncated form of the old term "pro-choice" (itself a euphemism). The "pro" has been interdicted from accepted usage by the choice movement's lexicographers, presumably for reasons of pith. (Or perhaps for other reasons. As a fellow who worked for the rock group REO Speedwagon once remarked, explaining why the band had shortened its name to REO: "It's simpler, more elegant—and it's easier to spell.")

Thus it came as little surprise when the HWPC dispatched a contingent for what was sure to be *the* social event of the "choice" season: the March for Women's Equality/Women's Lives, held here over a weekend in mid-April. The starlets' every step in the nation's capital—and as a reporter I of course had to monitor each one closely—illustrated the ease with which the HWPC is able to move between the two different worlds of Hollywood and Washington. The HWPC contingent was 250 strong—a figure that does not include the obligatory cosmeticians, hairstylists, and speech coaches, nor the starlets' finely muscled, deeply tanned toy-boys who had come along for the ride but who for the most part remained on the periphery of the weekend's activities, thoughtfully chewing gum and trying to keep their hair in place.

Who then were the noble 250? "We are writers, we are actresses, we are camera people, we are producers, we are directors," announced Miss Tabankin shortly after the HWPC hit town, "and now we are here as enablers." One thing a contingent of TV actresses can enable, of course, is a packed press conference, and indeed the reporters were all but swinging from the Bakelite chandeliers in the Hyatt Regency's grand ballroom the afternoon before the march, when the HWPC starlets (and the producers, directors, etc., as if anybody cared about them) joined other march organizers to meet the Washington press. For purposes of publicity, naturally, it was the actresses who came to the fore. With great excitement the hacks huddled around Kelly McGillis and Jane Fonda, Veronica Hamel and Donna Mills, Cybill Shepherd and a dozen others I have seen during my ritualistic nightly viewing of *Entertainment Tonight*. Morgan Fairchild, who has donned her negligee for any number of evening soap operas and made-for-TV movies, was chosen as HWPC spokesstarlet for the Choice Weekend. (She also serves as "chair"—another easier-to-spell truncation—of the HWPC's busy "reproductive-freedom" subcommittee.) Head high, shoulders back, her golden hair falling in angelic cascades, she read a prepared statement about applying "our professional expertise and public visibility to effect political change." Her elocution was out of this world.

Later, during one of several "press availabilities," I asked Miss Fairchild about the HWPC. She said its role was—this should come as no surprise—"evolving." "In the past," she said, "we've raised a lot of money for candidates, but now we're moving into an issue focus, with an agenda that has a strategy." No wonder the starlets had the Washington press corps in a lather! This kind of statement would impress any reporter, however jaded. Here in the Beltway, as a matter of political etiquette, it is generally agreed that every third publicly spoken sentence must contain at least one of the following words: "issue," "bottom line," "agenda," "player," "strategy," "focus," or "articulate [verb form only]."* In using four of them in a single sentence—albeit a compound sentence—Miss Fairchild proved herself a Washington player of the very first rank; she even added, as a kind of lagniappe, that the "strategy was necessary to implement our feelings on choice." One HWPC member told me that, since Miss Fairchild's career in show business has lately been less than robust, there has been talk of her seeking elective office in a few years. More than a mere player, then: this woman could become another John Kerry.

Which would doubtless alarm the starlet-haters—who are, I repeat, sincere and honorable persons of good faith. Such purists are even to be found among the ranks of the pro-abortionists. A friend of mine, when she heard of the HWPC migration to Choice Weekend, complained that the starlets' presence would trivialize the cause. But think of it from the point of view of Beltway reporters: Wouldn't you rather lis-

---

* A corollary to this rule, incidentally, and one that applies only to men and women of the Left, requires that the phrase "in this country" be plopped into as many sentences as possible as often as possible, e.g., "The choice movement in this country is concerned above all with the quality of life in this country" (Marge Tabankin). With repeated use it becomes sort of a verbal hiccup, much as a congressman will use the phrase "quite frankly."

ten to drivel from Miss Fairchild or Donna Mills than from a
Washington regular like—well, like John Kerry, for example?
Or Ralph Nader? There may not be much in the package,
but what a package.

After her fine reading of HWPC's prepared statement, Miss
Fairchild was followed at the press conference by the Mammy
Yokum or the choice people, NOW's Molly Yard. The contrast was stunning. Morgan seduced the cameras with parted
lips and a sultry come-hither; Molly scowled. Morgan spoke
firmly, affecting intelligence. Molly raged into the mike, and
set the woofers in the PA to rumbling. Then came another
Washington regular, Faye Wattleton of Planned Parenthood,
who hollered that the Bush administration was not only
"putting the government on the backs of women but into our
reproductive organs as well"—an unbecoming metaphor
even for a sex educator. No one need worry about starlets
trivializing discourse in Washington. Given a low enough
cause, they can even elevate it.

Puff the Magic Dragon
Goes to Jail

March 1986

PETER, PAUL, AND MARY ADDED THEIR NAMES this January to the rolls of the more than three thousand "messengers" who have been arrested at the South African embassy on Massachusetts Avenue. Several others—Peter's daughter, Mary's daughter, Mary's mother, a rabbi, and some Unitarians—went along for the ride. To kick things off, the movement held a media event *cum* rally on a tree-lined side street half a block down from the embassy. Bishop Desmond Tutu showed up to give his blessing, which brought out scores of press people—as many press people, in fact, as protesters. My own reasons for going were part personal, part professional, but mostly personal. Fulfilling a fantasy I've had since I first heard "Puff the Magic Dragon," I just wanted to see Peter, Paul, and Mary get thrown in jail.

Before the rally began, I disdained the perks and access allowed me as a member or the media community and situated myself instead in front of a group of schoolgirls. The day was bitter cold, but the girls were having a wonderful time. They each wore a green armband (some wore two), and most carried signs that read, "Jerry Falwell doesn't speak for me." In the manner of young girls, their conversation was rapid-fire and giggly. One, about fourteen, admired another girl's sign, a broad, garish thing with an outline of South Africa on it. On its back was stamped: "Liberation Graphix." "That has got to be the cutest one I've seen," she said. "By far. It is so cute." The girl with the sign was obviously pleased but only shrugged. "You can get them anywhere," she said. Then, distracted by a mother pushing a stroller, she cooed, "Oh, look at that baby!" Another shouted, "Babies United Against Apartheid!" They began giggling. "Speaking of babies, where's Des baby? Des baby, where are yooooo?"

Bishop Tutu, as he is more widely known, arrived late, driving up the side street in the mayor's motorcade from the back way, out of the crowd's view. He sat in the limousine for several minutes, giving an exclusive interview to a reporter from the *Post*. Peter, Paul, and Mary and several other celebrities — Pat Schroeder, the left-wing congressman from Colorado, Roger Wilkins from the Institute for Policy Studies, and the ubiquitous Mary Frances Berry of the U.S. Civil Rights Commission—gathered round and bowed and shuffled in front of Tutu when he finally stepped out of the limo. As is their wont, the protesters began chanting to pass the time: "Apartheid's wrong / Let's sweep it away. / That's A-F-R [beat] I-C-A"; "Break the ties / [clap-clap-clap] / With apartheid." They finally settled on a simple antiphony, probably because the white people present (they were a majority here) had no trouble following it: "Freedom Yes! / Apartheid No!" I moved to the back of the crowd, next to a young couple who looked like they were skipping classes at Georgetown. The girl leaned with her back against a tree, her boyfriend leaned against her; she held him tight. She chanted "Freedom Yes!" and he threw his head back in a mighty grimace, bellowing, "Apartheid No!" The chant continued for a minute or two, until a frenetic climax. Loud cheers and applause followed, and the boy wheeled around, pinned the girl against the tree, and kissed her deeply.

She bent her knee slightly, taking him in as her right foot edged up the trunk of the tree.

Throughout all this, the press photographers—the shooters— grew impatient. Where was the action? Where was Tutu? They stood on a platform before the clump of microphones where the bishop would speak. "Bring him out, for Chrissake!" one photographer hollered. "What the hell are you waiting for?" Tutu eventually made his way through the crush of admirers, and as he emerged, the cameramen came alive. You could hear their motor drives whirring in the cold. They shouted belligerently at anyone who dared come between them and Tutu and interfere with the public's right to know. Before Tutu spoke, Mary implored everyone to sing along with "Blowing in the Wind"—"even you in the press!" A photographer behind me chuckled and in a sinister voice said, "You bet, honey." Not that it would have mattered; once the song began Mary was the only thing you could hear. The years have not been pleasant to the trio, especially Mary, who, though she still sports the trademark Roman helmet of straight blond hair, has taken on a few extra wrinkles, or maybe laugh lines, and a few dozen extra pounds. As she belted out the songs, she wagged her head and threw her body from side to side, while the other celebrities struggled to anchor themselves against the assault of her weight.

After Tutu's remarks, which were witty and brief, there were some concluding chants, and then the messengers boarded a beat-up school bus marked "First Rising Mount Zion Baptist Church" and were driven the half block to the embassy. The cops checked our press passes and allowed us to scramble up Massachusetts Avenue, where we could watch the arrest from across the street. In the embassy driveway, another dozen or so cops stood waiting by the open doors of a paddy wagon. "Hey, Clarence," one of the shooters called over the traffic, "before you put 'em in the wagon turn 'em towards us so we can get a good shot. Parade 'em around for a little bit. I'll love ya for life." The cop gave him a blank look and turned around and patted his rear end. "You love me?" he shouted over his shoulder. "Then give me a kiss right here." The messengers stepped off the bus and huddled round the door of the embassy. Paul Stookey said some words into the call box. "Oh come on, idiot," said a guy in front of me, holding his camera aloft. "Just get it over with." "What do you care?" said another shooter. "You're probably out of film anyway." "I'm not as dumb as I look, asshole." "No. Nobody's that dumb." "Oh, yeah?" said the first fellow. "What about these guys?" The messengers got no response from inside the embassy, so they slowly walked to the parkway in front of us, arms intertwined, faces aglow, and began singing "We Shall Overcome": Paul, Peter and his daughter, the Unitarians, the rabbi, and in the middle, Mary's daughter, Mary's mother, and Mary, swaying her great body to and fro. A cop with a bullhorn gave them one perfunctory warning, then another. "Oh, sing it, mama!" said the shooter in front of me, his camera to his eye. "Sing it, you big fat pig!" One by one the cops gently helped them, still singing, into the paddy wagon.

Jesse Jackson's
Old Pals

May 1988

THE MAINSTREAMING OF JESSE JACKSON HAS
been one of the recurrent stories of the presidential campaign,
popping up every couple of primaries or so, and his new
"moderation" is held to be the reason for his recent success-
es. Over the past few months Jesse has proved that in Democratic primaries he can sweep the black vote and pull down
somewhat less than 10 percent of the white liberal vote, which
makes him, as the media like to put it, "viable": meaning that
in a national election—if he retained his iron grip on these
constituencies—he would only lose by a margin of about 65
percent.

How to account for Jackson's development as a states-
man—his rise to viablenesshood? The sufficient cause has
been an adoring press, speckled with passages like this one
from Paul Taylor, a first-stringer on the *Washington Post*'s
campaign staff: "The more Jackson achieves, the more
movingly he is able to chronicle the journey that got him
there—as a parable, he says, 'for what is best about America.'
And when he has told audiences this week, 'When I win, we
can all win,' he has brought goosebumps, throat lumps, tears
of joy and the gift of hope—and not just to blacks."

Taylor was writing from the press section, where the
"goosebumps and throat lumps" (the master's impressive

poesy is rubbing off) are probably in abundance; but dispatches composed in such caldrons of high emotion are usually incomplete. In referring to "the journey that got him there," for example, Taylor doesn't mention that Jesse hasn't done an honest day's work in twenty years—a record even more impressive than that of professional "public servants" like Bob Dole and Richard Gephardt. Jesse's own Horatio Alger story has been realized by means that require less discipline and less energy: squeezing tithes from middle-class blacks, mau-mauing corporate liberals, conspiring with federal bureaucrats, shaking down television stations for thousands of hours of free (and highly sympathetic) coverage, and so on. Maybe that's what Jesse means when he says, "I'm a tree-shaker, not a jelly-maker." Then again, maybe not.

There's a second reason for Jesse's baptism in the mainstream, one for which he himself is more directly responsible. With a degree of difficulty we will never know, he has kept his most obvious impulses to radicalism in check, largely by freeing himself of guilt by association. There have been no more trips to Syria and ("Viva Fidel!") Cuba. Bert Lance, always considered a moderate Democrat, is now his closest campaign adviser. The wife—even more radical than Jesse—has been staying home. No more valentines to Arafat. And most conspicuously, there have been no more bear hugs for Minister Louis Farrakhan, the Nation of Islam leader who proved so inconvenient in 1984.

Farrakhan came to Washington recently, appearing at the University of the District of Columbia on a double bill with Dr. Lenora Fulani, another early Jackson supporter who is now running for president herself, as an independent—"the first African-American woman ever to qualify for federal primary matching funds." Farrakhan had been invited by the UDC student government, which agreed to pay him $7,500, plus $1,000 in expenses. This figure struck some people as rather a high price to pay an anti-Semitic lunatic for a two-hour rave-up, and there was controversy. I was glad, however, when the protests failed to cause the students to rescind the invitation, because I was eager to reconnoiter the boosters who launched Jesse in 1984 but whom he has now jettisoned, like spent fuel, as he soars into respectability. It's a mistake I won't make twice.

UDC is only ten years old, and its buildings, designed during that unfortunate lagtime of the post-Bauhaus, prepostmodernist mid-seventies, are angled together from slabs of poured concrete. Farrakhan and Dr. Fulani were to speak in the gymnasium, atop a hill overlooking Connecticut Avenue. It's an austere building, relieved only by small terraces jutting out at various levels along the outer walls. As I climbed the hill I noticed that on each terrace burly young black men were standing at attention. Each had the trademark close-cropped haircut, and each wore the Nation of Islam uniform: black double-breasted suit with padded shoulders, freshly pressed white shirt, and extra-small bright-red bow tie. The closer I got the more of them I saw, until, entering the gym through the press entrance, I had counted upward of fifteen. Inside the gym there were many more. Under such a circumstance, Farrakhan's fee seemed more than reasonable: $7,500 wouldn't buy these big guys *lunch*.

In a holding area inside the gym one of the bodyguards gave me an expert body search, and confiscated my miniature Swiss Army knife with the four different functions. I'm unsure what he thought the danger was—maybe I was planning to charge the stage and hurl the minister to the ground and trim his fingernails—but whatever friendliness the guards were inclined to show evaporated about then. They ushered me into the gym and set me in the first row, directly in front of the stage where Farrakhan would speak.

With a half hour to show time, the gym was still half empty; the crowd arrived in a trickle through the bottleneck created by the friskers at the front door. I struck up a conversation with a couple of photographers who were milling around— a play for the kind of amused, another-day-another-dollar chitchat common to reporters at such events, an act of Fourth Estate solidarity. I thought it might loosen up the tight ball of uneasiness beginning to form in my stomach.

"We'll be lucky if they start this thing in an hour," one of them told me. "I saw him in Madison Square Garden, and they searched every one of the 35,000 people. I was afraid I was going to be there all night."

He asked me who I was writing for and I told him but I don't think it registered, which is just as well. He turned to the other photographer. "I saw somebody from the Jewish press outside," he said. "Can't you just see what he's writing? 'Louis Farrakhan stormed into Washington tonight, spewing his hatred and anti-Jewish propaganda throughout this predominantly Negro city. . . .'" He shook his head and chuckled. "Shit. Those people . . ."

The tight little ball got a little tighter, and I took my seat again. Presently the place filled. The crowd was mostly students, attired in the student manner: blue jeans and backpacks, with Jackson buttons and Doug Williams T-shirts much in evidence. There was a smattering of old people, and a generous helping of young professionals, dressed for an evening out. From my front-row seat I made a quick survey of the hall and noticed—contrary to my better instincts—that there were no more than a half-dozen white faces sprinkled throughout, not counting a camera crew at the very rear of the gym.

To begin we rose and sang the black national anthem, which, on first hearing at least, is even less tuneful than "The Star-Spangled Banner." Farrakhan hadn't yet arrived, but Dr. Fulani, the New Alliance candidate for president and recipient of $300,000 in federal matching funds, killed time with a thirty-minute address that outlined her "Two Roads

Are Better Than One" strategy for blowing a little sunshine into the white male power structure.

The First Road, she said, is Jesse's. "I am a staunch supporter of Reverend Jesse Jackson" and his "profoundly moral vision for our people," she said. But something had happened with Jesse. "When someone runs for the presidency, he or she typically asks other leaders for their endorsement. . . . It is striking, therefore, that the two black leaders whom you have invited to speak to you today have not been sought out by Jesse Jackson and asked to stand by him."

Not that there are any hard feelings. "I must make clear that I don't take this personally," she said, even though "it might seem as if Jesse has gone out of his way not to call upon us, or even to look in our direction." He can cozy up to the "white supremacist Democratic party leadership" all he wants to, and if he's the nominee, which she doubts, "I would immediately withdraw my candidacy and put all the resources of my independent campaign at his disposal."

Jesse himself might be moved by this gesture, but Dr. Fulani's generosity probably wouldn't be any great help to a mainstream, viable campaign with all the trimmings; her federal matching funds would scarcely cover Bert Lance's bar tab at the Democratic convention. Nevertheless, the offer's on the table. And if the Rev's not nominated, there's always the Second Road: she will continue her candidacy "as our insurance policy that the black vote will not be taken for granted."

Dr. Fulani was respectfully received—she eventually got a standing ovation, in fact, but this was a pushover crowd. The minister was the draw, and in time his arrival was heralded by seven very large men—a cookie-cutter vision in the double-breasted suits, the padded shoulders, the white shirts, the little bow ties—who marched with military precision to the front of the stage and stood at attention until the minister was safely at the podium. Then they fell to at-ease.

* * *

Farrakhan is disconcertingly boyish: plump even, with eyes
that twinkle behind his wire-rimmed glasses and a snaggle-
toothed grin. But when he begins to speak—which wasn't
for some time, since his ovation was prolonged—the boy-
ishness vanishes. In conversational tones his voice sounds
like HAL the computer, from the movie *2001*. But when it
rises to exhortation or censure it evokes an angry sob. As
he prowls the stage he is silken. When he speaks of Allah,
his body curves back taut like a bow; when he speaks of the
white man it descends to a feral crouch and the head shakes
and the arms flail the air. Throughout it all a phalanx of five
bodyguards follows him in tight formation, shifting this way
when he moves to his right, reassembling that way when he
moves to his left—sort of like the Pips, by way of the Marine
Corps.

The crowd was his from the beginning. The torrent of bad
publicity that attended his invitation made a fortress of the
gym: here on the inside were his people, and on the outside
were the *Washington Post* and the "good blacks" and the
media and the white people—not *all* the white people, of
course, for there was at least one on the inside, in the very
front row as a matter of fact, who was becoming increasingly self-conscious. "All the scholars who are here," said
Farrakhan, "and the scientists and the historians: pay good
attention and critically appraise what Farrakhan has to say.
They're angry that you've come, that you waited in line to
see and hear and meet your brother." And what's more, *they*
had turned off the air conditioning. (I hadn't noticed.)
"They're trying to make you uncomfortable so you won't
pay attention to the cool words you're about to hear." At
this slight provocation the assembly rose as one and let out
hollers of "Tell it!" and "Say the word!"

He spoke on education. "When you're arrogant," said Farrakhan, "you think you already know, and when you think you already know, you stop thinking, and when you stop thinking, you stop seeking, and when you stop seeking you stop growing, and when you stop growing you stop living and when you stop living you start dying and death grows all around you with this arrogant attitude." These hipbone-connected-to-the-thighbone flourishes recur in the minister's discourse, and as they pile up they become impossible to follow. They didn't seem to bother the audience, though, which responded, so far as I could tell, to subverbal cues: whoops would issue from the scholars and scientists and historians with each break in his creamy delivery, and at those moments when the words started rushing fast and loud the crowd would heave and rumble like a thundersquall. He could have been reciting the phone book. Such discontinuity between action and reaction happens everywhere in American politics; Jackson gets the same response from the ADA. Besides, this was a modern American university; it wasn't the sort of lecture where they give you a quiz later.

The subject of education led to the subject of character, which led, on an upward spiral of intensity, to the subject of Farrakhan and his critics, specifically his white critics. "Everything you've tried to do to thwart the rise of Farrakhan," said Farrakhan, "is meeting a resistance that you didn't think was there, because you aren't equipped to go beyond what you've been taught and trained. . . . You can't handle it because you're stuck where you are with that racist, white supremist mentality. You hate me!" The crowd erupted like Krakatoa. I looked up from scribbling furiously on my notepad and was startled to see Farrakhan crouched on the stage right in front of me. I suddenly realized he was talking to *me*. "I'll tell you— you and all White America—I've got the key to let you out of the prisons of the sickness of your mind. [Big cheers!] And if you doubt me, try me. I know the origin of your mind, I know where your thoughts arise from. We have an *absolute* knowledge of white people!" Goosebumps, throat lumps: the bodyguards snapped to attention again. "White people are locked in the prison of a mind that represents death, and if the key is not applied, you will destroy yourselves and be *destroyed* by *God* in the New World that is coming even now!"

Even now! Like tonight! Against my better judgment I wheeled around to catch the eye of a white couple several rows behind me. They were sitting stiffly amid the frenzy and staring straight ahead and smiling to beat the band, in a goofy, Alfred E. Neuman sort of way. The woman next to me was bouncing up and down and yelling, "That's right!" I understood his point about the air conditioning. "Can you imagine these white writers who have the [here he fell into an Etonian accent] un-mit-i-gat-ed gall to call me—a victim of white racism, a victim of *your* bigotry—and you call me a bigot? When you yourself are the standard—the *standard*—of everything you accuse me of? You have that audacity? We have done no evil to you!"

He was still in front of me. I could have yelled, "Right! I agree! I agree! Now get off my case!" But it would have sounded hopelessly white, and no one would have heard me anyway. Slowly the crowd quieted, and he continued, in his HAL voice: "We cleaned your floors. Remember? And when you asked us, 'You do windows, don't you?' we said yes. We left our homes unclean to clean yours. We left our children unkept to keep your children." He straightened from his crouch and started prowling again, raising the roof. "When you were our managers, our agent, you kept the money, we got the change. You run the institutions. You're the *screenwriter*, the Hollywood *promoter*, who made us Little Black Sambo, Stepin Fetchit, made us buck-and-wing dancers and clowns while you pulled the strings of our women! You wrote the textbooks that made us hate ourselves and murdered our history with your lies, your lies, *your lies!*"

"Liar!" the woman to my left yelled at me. "You still telling your lies! Liar!" I remember noticing she had an "All Things Considered" bookbag at her feet, but that's about all—my eye for the reportorial detail was sliding shut. I did look down the row past the woman, searching for my photographer buddy, my Fourth Estate pal, but he was standing with his arms raised, hollering, "Tell the truth!"

Things eventually leveled off, although the air conditioner never came back on. The minister later mentioned Jackson briefly—which is what I'd come to hear, after all—saying that Jesse was finally drawing support from white folk, those who had "been made humble by suffering." "Here comes their white knight," he said, "only he's black! But if you're in a burning house, dying of smoke inhalation, you don't care if the fireman who's coming to rescue you is black or white."

I wonder: Do Paul Kirk and his fellow Democratic honchos feel they're being rescued? Now that they're all agreed on Jesse's new moderation, the preoccupying question has become, "What does Jesse want as a reward?" The consensus seems to be: include a few of his favorite planks in the platform, toss a Cabinet post or two to his cronies, maybe give Bert back his old table at Duke Zeibert's. They're assuming that as Jesse strides closer to the inner sanctum of Democratic power, the more he distances himself from his past—from Farrakhan and Dr. Fulani and their extremely enthusiastic followers. But from what I can see, his old buddies are sidling up right behind him. Some friends you just can't shake.

Trust Us: The Mystery
of the Supreme Court

November 1993

WHY IS THAT SUPREME COURT JUSTICES HARDLY ever appear in cheesy Washington dramas? Consider the stock characters of this beloved genre: the dipso southern senator, the avuncular secretary of state, the right-wing military man, the hormonally supercharged congressman, the network-news twinkie, the stolid editor-in-chief . . . not a Supreme Court justice in the bunch.

But why? In 1981, a movie starring Walter Matthau and Jill Clayburgh tried to correct the oversight, and in so doing indirectly answered the question. *First Monday in October* is the best movie ever made about the Supreme Court and is, in fact, the only movie ever made about the Supreme Court. The producers strove mightily to convey the court's constitutional grandeur. Handel's *Water Music* washes over the audience whenever the screen shows the court's temple-headquarters on First Street in Washington. But when the camera moves inside, all efforts at verisimilitude are self-defeating. Walter mugs, Jill looks implausibly thoughtful; but the truth is that nothing much happens. The movie bombed. Not even Miss Clayburgh's performance as the first female justice of the Supreme Court required to do a shower scene could redeem its dramatic shortcomings.

The title *First Monday in October* refers to the opening date of the court's annual term. When it convened last month, court watchers held out hope for some real-life drama at last. The occasion marked the first appearance of Justice Ruth Bader Ginsburg, the second woman appointed to the court and the first Democratic appointee in twenty-five years. In the event, however, Justice Ginsburg's star appeal was more on the order of Imogene Coca than Jill Clayburgh. Nothing, it turned out, can overcome the tedium of a session of the Supreme Court.

Tedium is what the justices prefer. This is why they're so dangerous.

In his book *The Supreme Court: How It Was, How It Is*, Chief Justice William Rehnquist called the court "one of the best tourist sights in Washington." No one will confuse it with the National Museum of Air and Space, but unsuspecting tourists come by the busload anyway. On days the court is in session, the queue snakes across the plaza and down the block.

As the crowds wait to enter, the temple looms above them as a mood setter, a symbol of ageless power and indestructibility meant to suggest the Parthenon, which was blown up by Turks. The court does only a small portion of its business in public: during oral arguments, held Mondays, Tuesdays, and Wednesdays of the first two weeks of every month from October through April, and on days when its opinions are handed down, through June. Cameras and recording devices are not allowed, in keeping with the cloistered professional lives the justices otherwise lead. They never hold press conferences, rarely give speeches, and seldom, during business hours, venture out of the sealed-off corridors of the temple, which they reach through an underground parking garage and private elevator.

The conceit is that justices are removed from the whirlwinds and tidal waves of democratic government, a rare breed whose eyes rise above popular passion, elevated always to the Law. The opening ceremony is meant to augment this sense of mystery and majesty. The unwashed pass through metal detectors and massive bronze doors to the chamber itself, a marble room built to the dimensions of a college gym but with worse acoustics and no cheerleaders. Impossibly tall curtains of red plush fall between twin columns of white marble. A frieze depicting lawgivers through the ages adorns the upper walls. There is much brass and gold brocade. It looks like a set from *Samson and Delilah*.

In the center of the chamber is a large area for lawyers of the bar; the press sits in an apse to one side. Spectators are rotated in and out in small groups every few minutes as the session progresses. Their seating area, farthest from the bench, holds about two hundred. Guards circumnavigate it with the bullying air of hall monitors. A whap of the gavel, and the curtains part behind the bench, and the justices enter in groups of three. The clerk hollers: "Oyez, oyez, oyez! [legalese for "Soup's on!"] The Honorable, the Chief Justice and the Associate Justices of the Supreme Court of the United States. All persons having business before this Honorable Court are admonished to draw nigh and give their attention, for the court is now sitting. God save the United States and this Honorable Court."

By the time the clerk finishes, the justices are seated, and the tourists have their first good look at them. "I know of no other regularly scheduled occasion," the chief justice wrote in his book, "on which strangers to the Nation's Capital can be guaranteed a view of so many persons responsible for the functioning of one of the three branches of the United States government." It is a salutary guarantee but ironic: As you watch the faces of these assembled Americans, fresh off the tour bus, it is clear that not one of them has the slightest idea who these nine people are. Most consult seating charts provided by the court. Not even Clarence Thomas, star of one of the highest-rated shows in television history, seems to rouse a flicker of recognition. I noticed a frisson pass through the crowd only once, when Nina Totenberg came in late.

You can't fault the public for its ignorance. The justices are not a particularly noteworthy bunch. Their black robes are another suggestion of majestic imperturbability, creating the illusion that beneath each austere cloak beats the heart of a legal giant. The illusion is crucial, for without the robes most of the justices look as if they were gathered at random from the nearest shuffleboard court. In fact, they were recruited from the swamps of American politics—either electoral politics or, what is even less promising, the politics of the American legal establishment.

By tradition, an appointment to the Supreme Court rewards a long career of bar-association schmoozing, political hack work, and assiduous bum bussing. The only current exceptions to the rule are Justices Ginsburg and Antonin Scalia. Both had distinguished legal careers before coming to the court—Scalia as a scholar and Ginsburg as a skilled and creative litigator. A quick glance at their colleagues shows less impressive qualifications.

At the far end of the bench sits Justice Thomas, perhaps the most famous person in the court after Nina Totenberg. The politics of his appointment to succeed the court's first black justice, Thurgood Marshall, need little elaboration—it was, said the press and others, selection by quota, which Thomas opposes on constitutional grounds. Next to Thomas is Anthony Kennedy, who came to the court after a languid career as a law professor at a third-tier law school and several years on a federal appeals court, where his tough-on-crime opinions drew the attention of Reaganites. He was President Reagan's third choice to fill the seat.

As a presidential candidate hungry for women's votes in 1980, Reagan pledged that his first Supreme Court appointment would be a woman. When the chance came, he reached deep into the nation's judiciary, all the way down to an intermediate state court of appeals in Arizona, to find Sandra Day O'Connor, an old friend of Rehnquist's, an acolyte of Reagan's mentor Barry Goldwater, and a good soldier in the state's right-wing politics . Next to her sits the court's oldest justice, Nixon appointee Harry Blackmun, who came to the court as a close friend of then-Chief Justice Warren Burger. President Nixon knew Burger, in turn, because Burger was once Harold Stassen's campaign manager. Of all the credentials that have ensured justices a place on the Supreme Court, Blackmun's may be the most dubious: the friend of a friend of Harold Stassen's.

In the center sits Chief Justice Rehnquist, appointed to the court by Nixon after a long career as a lawyer–political activist in Arizona and a briefer career in John Mitchell's Justice Department, which eventually gave us Watergate. Reagan made him chief justice. Next is Justice John Paul Stevens, brought to President Ford's attention by then-Attorney General Ed Levi, who had enjoyed many pleasant bar-association conventions with Stevens.

Justice David Souter, to Scalia's left, was plucked from obscurity by John Sununu. As governor of New Hampshire, Sununu had appointed Souter to the state Supreme Court in return for Souter's lengthy servitude at the feet of New Hampshire's Republican pols. He may be the only man in Washington who doesn't regret sucking up to Sununu; at least he still has a job.

Next to Souter, at the far end of the bench, sits Justice Ginsburg, but it is Souter who embodies the modern court. Beyond his experience as a political coat-holder, his chief qualification was that no one could tell whether he was qualified or not. Some cynics dubbed him the "Stealth nominee." Before settling on Souter, the Bush administration did consider nominating judges and scholars of distinction. But the idea was quickly dismissed.

Their paper trails—articles and written opinions that indicate an intellectual engagement with constitutional issues—disqualified them as "too controversial," particularly for confirmation in a Democratic-controlled Senate. With his brief career on the state bench, Souter was, like most of his colleagues, blessedly unburdened by any evidence of distinction. Even better, he had for years lived in a cabin in the woods, far from the fleshpots where even the most timid lawyers can sometimes be lured into indiscretions that might haunt them as nominees. Phlegmatic, average, politically well-connected: Souter comfortably took a place among his peers.

After brief formalities, oral arguments begin. The court receives petitions to hear more than 6,000 cases a year but agrees to hear arguments in fewer than 150. An hour is set aside for each case, with the time split between the two sides. The lawyers already have filed their briefs, which the justices are presumed to have read. In these the arguments are presented entire; the oral presentations make the lawyers available for grilling by the justices.

The degree of interest each justice displays varies from case to case. Thomas is famously silent; since he's been on the court, he has asked only a handful of questions during oral arguments. He leans far back in his chair, folds his hands in front of his face, occasionally makes notes, and sometimes consults law books he keeps on the bench. Harry Blackmun is almost as quiet; his frequent yawns—great, languorous yawns that cause every feature on his face to recede into invisibility—have become the stuff of legend.

The chatterboxes are justices Souter and Scalia. Souter's face is long and drawn, Scalia's round and puckish. Both have five o'clock shadows, and side by side they look like the bad guys in a Dick Tracy cartoon. Scalia's manner is ferocious. He seems the sort of fellow who would snap, "Buy a paper!" if you asked him for a football score. He commonly begins a question with the pitiless formulation: "You aren't *really* trying to argue that. . ."

Souter, with his courtly New Hampshire manner and accent to match—"lawr" for law, "ahgument" for argument—is more decorous but less intelligible. He favors colloquialisms that can only confuse the attorneys before him: "I see you've put all your eggs in the warrant basket," he told one lawyer. "You're now in the nonnegotiable driver's seat," he knowingly told another, who looked as though he'd never dreamed he was in any such place.

To this short list of talkers, we may now add Justice Ginsburg. In a speech this summer, she warned of her fondness for questions. "I will have to be more restrained," she promised. "I'll have to do some self-censorship." Too late. She censored herself for precisely 9 minutes in her debut, then uncorked seventeen questions, many of them lengthy, in the next 51 minutes, for an average of one every 180 seconds—impressive considering that there were at least seven other justices trying to get a word in edgewise.

Souter's dithering, Scalia's law-professor peevishness, and Ginsburg's motor-mouth peppering combine to create a fearsome fusillade. Lawyers have been known to wither—even those who prepare several hundred hours for just this moment, as most do. A lawyer is lucky to get an uninterrupted minute before a justice prods him for clarification or amplification. Thereafter he answers questions without letup. Seeing one of these poor fellows melt before the bench in a puddle of humiliation can break your heart—until you remember he's a lawyer.

In theory an oral argument sounds like a dramatic occasion, but for the layman it's more like a foreign movie without subtitles. The participants speak in a language unknown to ordinary Americans—the code of a cult, crafted over centuries to obscure the obvious and thereby preserve the exclu-

sivity of the legal profession and guarantee its enormous fees.
After a while it all begins to take on a dreamlike quality:

> JUSTICE GINSBURG (intensely): Would any cognizable analogue
> to the *Croson* test still have a demonstrable impact on the
> federal fisc?
> LAWYER: Well, Your Honor, the scope of remedies available
> is incorporated, if only by inference, into the *de jure* dupli-
> cative burdens that fall on respondent.
> JUSTICE SOUTER (airily): But—hmmm—if you've met those
> *Jingles* preconditions—maybe I'm wrong—while ignoring
> your own *Zimmer* affirmations, then you've only proved
> cohesion and not compactness . Haven't you? Or am I wrong?
> LAWYER: I agree, Your Honor. The vacature case depends on
> whether a nonmutual collateral estoppel is adduceable from
> the retroactivity claim.
> JUSTICE SCALIA (peeved): You're joking! How do you apply a
> GELA remedy if those conditions obtain? You act as if this
> is a maximalization case!!

For all the spectators know, by the time everybody's
through the justices have made Urdu circumcision rites mandatory in public schools. When you watch the Supreme
Court, much has to be taken on faith. This is by design. Like
a filibustering senator, the justices have learned the tactical
uses of boredom. Sooner or later, in every book written about
the Supreme Court, you come across a quote from Alexander
Hamilton: The court, he said, is "the least dangerous branch
of government." Lawyers press the theme in articles for the
popular press: "The Least Dangerous Branch: Nothing to
Worry About." "It's No Big Deal, Honest: Reflections on
Hamilton's 'Least Dangerous Branch.'" And so on. But lawyers are as contentious as they are sneaky. When they all start
assuring us of the same thing, we're entitled to grow suspicious.

Though it nurtures an image of otherworldliness, the Supreme Court is a Washington political institution, smaller and less bureaucratic than most but sharing with all such institutions a thirst for aggrandizement and power. It was not always so. In the beginning, the justices resembled a band of itinerants. They rode circuit in fall, winter, and spring, visited Washington for two sessions of two or three weeks'duration in August and February, and retired to their homes for the balance of the year. For most of the court's life, it even lacked its own building. The justices were shunted from room to room in the Capitol and even met occasionally in a friendly tavern. They seemed not to mind. When Congress, in 1896, offered to move them to a permanent court in the newly completed Library of Congress building, they unanimously rejected the invitation.

Then came Chief Justice (and former president) William Howard Taft, whose conception of the court's grandeur and importance was as vast as . . . William Howard Taft. The pompous temple on First Street was his idea, though its construction proceeded under his successor, Charles Evans Hughes. The court took up residence there in 1935. When the sculptor Robert Aitken was commissioned to design the frieze above the entryway, he made sure its giant, mythic figures bore the likenesses of Hughes, the architect Cass Gilbert (who had hired him), and himself. As it turns out, they all look like Hulk Hogan. But it was a fittingly vain gesture for a building that is, at bottom, a monument to institutional vanity.

The court's intellectual history shows the same relentless aggrandizement. Spending so much time on a set from *Samson and Delilah*, the justices begin to think of themselves as Victor Mature (or Hedy Lamarr) . For most of this century, the court has removed ever larger areas of American life from the discretion of elected representatives and the public, substituting its own preferences for theirs. As former politicians, justices cannot resist the temptation to make policy.

The most obvious examples came in the 1950s and '60s. The Warren Court's hunger for power was breathtaking. It refashioned American culture according to the whims of its justices, and in ways that no elected representative, having to face the electorate, would dare propose. Some of these were changes for the better, some weren't; but whether the court—unelected, unaccountable, and irreversible—had the right to make them is highly dubious. The justices redrafted welfare-eligibility requirements, redrew congressional districts, rewrote the lesson plans of public school teachers, and much, much else. Always they took care to swaddle their power grabs in constitutional finery, discovering rationales in the founding document's unwritten "spirit" or "evolution," the details of which seemed discernible only to those blessed with a law degree.

The Rehnquist Court is slightly more modest. It makes the most of the boredom it induces in laymen, usually avoiding a sweeping Warren-like decision in favor of incremental reform. But it, too, fiddles with any public policy it wants, from the shape of congressional districts to smoking restrictions in penitentiaries. In the words of one scholar, "its reaction to nearly any problem is to enhance its own policy discretion . . . case by case to achieve what it believes to be desirable social results."

Achieving "desirable social results," of course, is supposed to be the business of elected representatives. If they achieve an undesirable social result, we can vote them out of office. That's democracy. But we can't get rid of Supreme Court justices. The Constitution grants them life tenure—one of the few constitutional provisions they take literally.

It is a dilemma as old as democracy itself: What to do when a branch of government runs amok? Normally the press acts as a check on the power-crazed. Not in this instance. Perhaps reporters are blinded by the court's hauteur, or thrilled by its spirit of social reform; perhaps the unceasing boredom has done them in. Whatever the reason, Supreme Court reporters are remarkably uncritical when the justices grab more power. And any relinquishing of power, conversely, is condemned as an abdication of responsibility.

Two cases illustrate the tendency. In 1992 the court ruled that the beating of a prisoner by guards violated the Constitution's stricture against "cruel and unusual punishment." Justice Thomas dissented. He agreed that the beating was contemptible but pointed out that there were other legal remedies available, civil and criminal. The case did not raise a constitutional question, in Thomas's view, and thus was beyond the court's jurisdiction. The majority ruling, he wrote, "was yet another manifestation of the pervasive view that the Federal Constitution"—hence the court—"must address all ills in our society." Right or wrong, the intellectual distinction Thomas drew wasn't hard to comprehend. It was a rare decision—a justice admitting that the court could not assume control of every social question by claiming a constitutional prerogative. Press accounts suggested that Thomas was now in favor of beating convicts. For this the *New York Times* called him "the youngest, cruelest Justice."

Thomas may yet learn from Anthony Kennedy, whom the press hailed a year later for his very different kind of decision in *Lee v. Weisman*. In it the court ruled that nonsectarian prayers would be banned from public school graduation ceremonies. *Lee* was a classic court power grab: From its temple in Washington it reached uninvited into every high school gym and assembly hall in America and wagged its big finger like a two-by-four. Why? Kennedy offered an almost untraceable line of constitutional and psychological reasoning, which culminated in the unspoken words: Because I say so. It mattered not at all that the court itself opens with a kind of prayer, beseeching God to save it. Or that Congress does the same thing. Justice Kennedy had torn off the straitjacket of judicial restraint, and *Legal Times* praised his newly discovered "hankering to be fair."

Of course, reporters do not react to the Supreme Court with identical biases; if they did, readers might find their stories easier to follow. When last year's term drew to a close, several newspapers surveyed the court's decisions. "High Court's Term Shows No Drift to Center," headlined the *St. Louis Post-Dispatch*. "For High Court, a Term of Moving to Middle," responded *USA Today*. And the *New York Times* had it both ways: "Court's Counterrevolution Comes in Fits and Starts."

If the press can't control the court, who will? Reformers have suggested opening up its processes to public scrutiny. They point to Congress, with its C-SPAN–monitored deliberations, as an exemplar. The idea should give pause. Congress is in many ways a model of openness, but at a cost. You have only to see Bob Dornan howling before the cameras on the floor of the House, or watch congressmen prostrate themselves before a piece of sitcom cheesecake testifying on the destruction of the rain forest, to measure the price of openness. A showboating congressman is just an annoyance; a showboating justice can be dangerous.

In fact, the Supreme Court cocoon is quite permeable as it is. One former Supreme Court clerk speaks of the concentric circles that surround the court. The inner circle is the court itself, peopled exclusively by lawyers. Every term a justice hires four clerks (Stevens makes do with three) to research cases and draft opinions. The clerks are freshly graduated from the nation's top law schools, where, following the fashions of law professors, they have learned that justices are most ennobled when they take up the work of social reform that the lumbering public ignores.

Their power is by all accounts enormous. Although gossip routinely circulates about the influence of one clerk or another on individual justices, it is hard to know which stories to credit, since most of them originate with the clerks themselves. But clerks do decide, with minimal supervision, which cases the justices will hear among the thousands of petitions they receive. As a result, the court's docket fills with flashy cases involving sexual harassment, pornography, and racial discrimination, while less colorful though arguably more consequential issues in antitrust or trademark law go unheard. Few of the clerks have yet practiced law or even slaved at a real job, where they might learn the complications of work-aday life. They thus bring to the court the grad student's air of intellectualism and the twentysomething's taste for remaking the world. Neither trait is appropriate for the court of last appeal, but both influence its opinions.

Beyond this circle is the press. Their constant goading to judicial activism rivals that of the clerks, and has similar if less direct effects—at least one justice, Anthony Kennedy, reportedly has his clerks keep a scrapbook of his press clippings.

Then there is official Washington. The obsessions with politics and policy, celebrity and gossip, the imperiousness and elitism that detach Washington from the rest of the country become the ether in which the justices live and breathe. Though unrecognizable to most Americans, they are transformed by Washington alchemy into local celebrities. Dinner with Kay Graham, drinks with George Mitchell, racquetball with Ted Koppel: It is a long, inexorable seduction, an endless process of self-inflation, for which we all pay the price in the end.

One modest proposal suggests removing them from the Washington swamp altogether, by transplanting the court—

justices and clerks, law books and Xerox machines, the works—to Kansas City, say, or Billings, Montana, where they might reestablish contact with the public whose desires they routinely second-guess or override. The Supreme Court building itself could stand empty for a while, as a kind of monument to the perils of overweening government, and then be handed over to a local high school for basketball games.

But this proposal, while sound, is probably unworkable. The only antidote to a power-hungry Supreme Court, if there is one, will come from a different kind of justice—secure enough in his beliefs to resist the lure of Washington elitism, respectful enough of democratic process to keep her hands to herself. Such justices would be even more nondescript than the ones we have, and the Supreme Court, having relinquished its self-imposed role as policy maker, would become even more boring than it is. It would risk forgoing its status as "one of the best tourist sights in Washington," but no great loss: If the tourists wanted to see where policy is made, they could cross the street and watch congressmen bellow on the floor of the House—undignified and earthy, lacking robes and brocade, a spectacle, for better or worse, of democracy revived.

The Look That
Killed a Congressman

March 1994

CERTAIN FACIAL EXPRESSIONS ARE EMBEDDED
in our collective unconscious. Who can forget Mona Lisa's
creepy smile, or the forgiving resignation of Christ in Leo-
nardo's *Last Supper*? Who is not haunted by the visage of
Lee Harvey Oswald taking Jack Ruby's bullet, or of Jimmy
Carter pressing a sombrero around his ears on a state visit to
Mexico? Their faces capture for all time some wordless emotion or mystery or moment of pain. They are perdurable,
undis-missible, in the way of all archetypes. To this gallery I
would now like to add the look that crossed the face of the
Honorable Martin Hoke, Member of Congress for the Tenth
District of Ohio, as he prepared for a television interview one
evening in January 1994.

Perhaps this is the first you have heard of Martin Hoke.
Elected in 1992, when he unseated an eight-term incumbent,
he has settled for the national anonymity of the backbencher
while trying to appear indispensable to the folks back home.
Thus he stood in the Capitol's Statuary Hall following our
president's State of the Union speech, sweating almost imper-
ceptibly under the arc lights, as a live satellite feed was arranged
to beam his analysis to constituents waiting eagerly in Greater
Cleveland. He seemed, then, in those final moments, a self-
possessed man, a United States congressman comfortable in
his work.

What followed is not really a matter of dispute. A female producer approaches a congressman named Fingerhut, who is to be interviewed alongside Hoke. "Can I ask you to unbutton your jacket?" she asks Fingerhut, trying to wire him with a microphone.

"You can ask me to do anything you want," Fingerhut replies, striking an unmistakably salacious note.

She mikes Fingerhut, then Hoke, and disappears from the screen. Hoke glances at her, then at Fingerhut. He raises his hands slightly, cups them. And he says in an accent lifted from the Frito Bandito: "She has the *beeeega* breasts."

But that's not the most interesting part. For then the tape, with the masterly ease of a Truffaut, moves from the lowest comedy to the highest tragedy. Hoke gives Fingerhut a boyish grin and . . . freeze. The eyes still glisten, but from somewhere deep within the corneas they betray a dawning, unspeakable horror. The grin is fixed, but the tiny muscles around the mouth seem to be having spasms; neurons misfire.

He speaks. It is not a whisper. There is no frailty to the tone, for the vocal cords are still those of the man that Martin Hoke was just a few seconds before. They have not yet got the news that this Martin Hoke is ceasing to exist, being drained of life by a pitiless entropic force. His last words are: "We're probably live." The hands drop. The eyes narrow. Your heart breaks.

Here, in slow motion, is the look of one tripping headlong into the chasm that separates private thought from public behavior. As you watch him fall he gets smaller and smaller, until like Wile E. Coyote there is nothing left but a puff of smoke. Everyone leads a double life, of course; we say things to friends we would never say to strangers, and we think things we dare not say at all, unless we're Roseanne Barr. For the politician this condition is particularly acute, compounded and enlarged by the peculiar hypocrisies of his vocation. He must, in all circumstances, refrain from appearing to be a human being. The moment he enters public life, the Inner Frat Boy, who exists in all males, must be snuffed out. Failing to do this was Martin Hoke's crime, for which he was sentenced to death. In a literal sense, of course, a congressman named Martin Hoke lives on. But by his own admission, he is a New Man. Although his remark, as it happens, was not broadcast live, within days all of Cleveland had seen the tape. The inevitable sequence of events unwound.

His apologies were immediate and abject. "I deserve to get a two-by-four to the head," he said. He should have been so lucky! The well-endowed producer said she had not heard the beega remark as it was made, but: "I was disgusted." The hometown paper editorialized its rage: "Hoke does not seem to fathom that women who cross his line of sight are not merely body parts assembled for his viewing pleasure." Representatives of four local "women's groups" held a press conference: "We are asking him to seek sensitivity training on gender issues." A heretofore unknown woman surfaced with a year-old charge of sexual harassment. Six Democrats suddenly announced they would run against him. Hoke agreed to sponsor a town meeting "for women about women's issues," under the auspices of NOW.

His sentence, come to think of it, is worse than death. Chased by the acolytes of NOW, pelted with charges of sexual harassment, begging forgiveness from editorial writers: even the Puritans with their pillories were kinder. This is the fate that swam into view for Martin Hoke in those seconds of horror the videotape captured so pitilessly. Anyone who has seen it will not soon forget it, this archetype for the present age: the frozen aspect of a man about to be done in by boobs.

Don Imus's Sacrilege

April 1996

NOW MORE THAN A WEEK OLD, THE DON IMUS affair shows no sign of weakening its hold over Washington's moralists. This means that as an inside-the-Beltway obsession it has outlasted the North Korean nuclear crisis, the Steve Forbes surge, and the debt-ceiling extension combined. Only a true outrage can hold Washington's attention for such an eternity—a deliberate breach of some near-sacred precept. And indeed this is what Imus, for twenty-five years a famous New York radio entertainer, has committed. When he took the stage at the Radio and TV Correspondents Dinner on March 21, and made "inappropriate jokes" before the president and first lady, and forced his hosts to issue a general apology, and led White House press secretary Mike McCurry to ask C-SPAN not to rebroadcast his remarks, and caused soul-searching and brow-knitting among the worrywart community, Imus violated carefully tended standards and upended precious Washington rituals. For which he deserves a good deal of credit.

Like so many Washington controversies, the Imus affair was almost inevitable and yet utterly unexpected. Spring carries with it to Washington a round of press dinners—the Gridiron Dinner, the White House Correspondents Dinner, the

National Press Club Foundation Dinner, the White House
Photographers Dinner, the Radio and TV Correspondents
Dinner, and still more. These events follow a ritual as styl-
ized as a Kabuki or a High Mass, with fewer laughs.The ritual
unfolds like so. Members of the Washington press corps, or
some elite segment of it, gather in the ballroom of a downtown hotel to shower one another with praise: Awards are
bestowed for obscure accomplishments, tributes recited, fallen
comrades recalled. In this the press corps is like any other professional organization—say, the Council Bluffs chapter of the
American Association of Pre-owned Carpet Salespersons. The
difference is that the salesmen have the modesty and circum-
spection to keep the event within the fraternity; they do not,
for example, force invitations upon the people to whom they
have sold used carpet, under the presumption that anyone
would enjoy watching Paulie Luzzano accept his award for
High Volume Man of the Year.

The Washington press corps, of course, knows no such
modesty. For their annual fêtes, the newsfolk invite the people
they wrangle with and write about every day. They invite
politicians, and expect them to come. The politicians oblige,
almost without fail. And here is the essence of the ritual. Like
a mass, a press dinner is a reenactment, and as with a mass
its purpose is to reaffirm fundamental beliefs about the way
the world works. A religious ritual conjures from chaos the
proof that God's in His heaven and all's right with the world.
A Washington press dinner shows who's boss.

There shouldn't be any question about how the Washington
hierarchy is stacked. The president can strike down legisla-
tion, order men into battle, and annihilate whole cities with
the push of a button. Yet it is with trembling fingers and gnawing gut that he reaches each morning for the handiwork of
the Washington press corps. No, politicians understand as well
as anyone who carries the real power in Washington, and the

press dinner merely reifies the arrangement, acts it out and drives it home.

So invariably at press dinners the president is invited, and usually comes, and is made to grovel before his many-headed master. The preferred euphemism for "groveling" is "self-deprecation." By tradition, the president (or some surrogate—a vice president, a majority or minority leader) must show "he can laugh at himself." That is, the president must take the caricature of himself created by the press and use it as a template for his jokes: Thus President Reagan joked at press dinners about his absent-mindedness, his naps, his trigger-happy foreign policy; President Bush joked about being out of touch and to the manor born; Mrs. Reagan, in a performance that still brings hums of delight from pressfolk, humiliated herself by taking the stage at the Gridiron dressed in rags and warbling a parody of her high-flown tastes. A press don once said to me, "The Gipper may have been an idiot, but at least he and Nancy could laugh at themselves."

Self-deprecatory jokes can be very funny, but self-deprecation, when scripted by someone other than self, is simply eerie. As the president takes the podium, it is understood that he has had to haul in special talent to write the jokes—most administrations, in fact, keep a handful of professional joke writers on retainer for just this purpose—and this barely concealed fillip deepens the pleasure the audience derives from his humiliation. It is one thing for President Clinton to tell a joke about his large appetite; quite another when you realize the joke was concocted by a moonlighting Leno writer who was paid to sit and think about what a fatty the president is.

To be satisfactory, the politician's homily should contain two other elements. He must take a few mild jabs at his adversaries; and he must, in closing, lapse into sentimentality. As for the jabs, the essential word is "mild." Jokes at the expense of the press or Congress encourage the illusion of reciprocity: This president can give as good as he gets, by God. Of course, he cannot. If he did, the *Washington Post* Style section—which certifies these ceremonies the following morning—would point out that many of the politician's jokes were "barbed," or "crossed the line," or were "mean-spirited."

Consider the experience of Dan Quayle. Shortly after taking office, he stood in for President Bush at the White House Correspondents Dinner. John Tower's nomination as defense secretary had just been rejected by the Senate—and, of course, by the press—owing to his alleged boozing and womanizing. Quayle's first joke was: "Watching your conduct throughout the evening, I realized that most of you do not aspire to be secretary of defense."

"This was greeted by loud boos," the *Post* reported. Quayle's jokes, the paper stressed, were "barbed." They elicited groans from the press. "It gets better," Quayle told the crowd. The *Post* disagreed: "It didn't get much better."

Days later, Quayle appeared at the Gridiron. His opening joke, to everyone's relief, showed he had learned his lesson. Quayle said he had recently asked President Bush to make some public gesture that would demonstrate Bush's faith in his new vice president. The president, according to Quayle, put his arm around him and asked: "Do you want a puppy?" The joke was a big hit. Quayle was a big hit.

After the self-deprecation and the mild jabs, the politician caps his remarks with what sitcom writers call the "moment of shit," the syrupy summing up in which all that has gone before is cheerfully resolved. *A free press has served us pretty darn well for two hundred years. . . . Sure we have our differences, but we have the same goal in view, we share the same love of . . .* and so on. The First Amendment survives, the politician has subjugated himself, God's in His heaven, and all's right with the world.

But the press is not yet through with its politician-guest. The final segment of the ritual is "the entertainment," a monologue from a semi-famous, second-tier stand-up comic,

preferably one who is recognizable from TV: Paula Pound-
stone, Bill Maher, Al Franken, Conan O'Brien, Dennis Miller,
and suchlike. The comic too is expected to humiliate the
politician-guest, as well as throw in a safe gag or two about
the press (Sam Donaldson's loud mouth, Irving R. Levine's
bow ties). But because he will have gained his fame on network TV, he can be expected to joke comfortably within the
boundaries of taste set by delicate Washington sensibilities:
no sex jokes, no jokes about bodily processes, and so on. For
the most part the comics have complied.

And then somebody invited Imus.

As a 1990s disc jockey, Imus specializes in jokes about sex
and other bodily processes. But he is also famous for his political satire, much of it remarkably sophisticated, the rest of it
less so, but almost all of it funny. This has led dozens of journalists to appear regularly on his show—Cokie Roberts, Nina
Totenberg, Dan Rather, and many more—notwithstanding
that the political satire often overlaps with the sex and flat-
ulence jokes. Here is Imus at the outer edge, from a song
parody:

> She won't do housework, 'cause it makes her sick.
> Doesn't bake cookies like the rest of those chicks.
> The ace in her hole is a Willie that's slick
> That's why the First Lady is a tramp.

It should have come as no surprise, then, that Imus's monologue at the Radio and TV Correspondents Dinner was similarly tasteless. The surprise was how tasteless he wasn't. By
acclamation, the most offensive of his jokes concerned the
president's infidelity: "When Cal Ripken broke Lou Gehrig's
consecutive-games record, the president was at Camden
Yards . . . and we all heard the president holler, 'Go, Baby.'
And I remember commenting at the time, 'I bet that's not the

first time he's said that.' Remember the AstroTurf in the pickup?"

Many observers have blamed the dinner's organizers for inviting Imus, but in fact they were moving in uncharted territory. The rules of the ritual are getting confused. Imus makes remarkably crude jokes about the president and first lady on his radio show; then James Carville, George Stephanopoulos, Bob Bennett, Dee Dee Myers, and the president himself appear on it. Show-biz humor, including political jokes, has coincidentally been debased just as the office of the presidency follows a similar trajectory. Nowadays a man who wants to be president might confess his infidelity on *60 Minutes.* A man who *is* president might make jokes about his sex life and the seductive properties of AstroTurf in a public speech. He even might joke about his underwear before a televised audience of teenagers. It becomes harder and harder, therefore, for a press dinner to fulfill its assigned purpose of humiliation. The confluence of these trends led inevitably to Imus's performance at the podium of the correspondents' dinner.

Where Imus most seriously departed from the ritual, however, was in training his fire on the press itself. As noted, custom demands a few press jokes, the lamer the better. Imus told jokes that were funny and mean, and true: unforgivable. He recommended that Peter Jennings, a notorious ladies' man, have a V-chip installed in his shorts. He joked about the old charges of plagiarism that hover around Nina Totenberg, and Dan Rather's shaky mental health, and ABC News's devotion to the Clinton White House, and Ed Bradley's ludicrous earring ("Ed, you're a newsman, not a pirate"). At the High Mass of a press dinner, this isn't the stuff you're supposed to find in the missal. "If there was any real courage in that Washington press corps," said Scripps Howard's Martin Schramm, reflecting widespread indignation, "they would have walked out on Don Imus en masse." And damn the terrific vanilla bombe dessert.

* * *

Will the Imus affair do long-lasting damage to the press's
favorite ritual? The irony is that the president himself won't
let it. McCurry says the president looks forward to attending
the dinner next year, assuming he's reelected. And indeed he
is probably wise to make the promise.

It has taken many years for the press dinner to evolve to
this point. Incredibly, years ago, dinner organizers would
choose the entertainment *because the president might like it.*
President Eisenhower usually declined to attend the dinners;
only the promise of a performance by the Lennon Sisters,
fresh from the Lawrence Welk show, lured him out in his final
year in office. Barbra Streisand, a Kennedy favorite, was
invited to sing for JFK, and the torch singer Julie London was
used as LBJ bait.

The nature of the entertainment changed as the media
grew more adversarial, until the evening blossomed into the
full-blown unpleasantness that the press enjoys today. Presi-
dents balk, but they pay a price. Jimmy Carter may have
fainted while jogging and joked about diarrhea during state
visits, but he had enough understanding of the presidency's
inherent dignity to hate press dinners. He skipped more than
he attended—further evidence, reporters said, that "he didn't
like the press." (To which the only answer is: "What's to
like?") And a former staffer recalls coaching President Bush
before his performance at a press dinner. "I don't want to do
this," Bush finally said. "I will not do this."

"You have to do it," the staffer replied.

"But I'm president of the United States!" Bush said. "I don't
have to do it if I don't want to."

"Mr. President," the staffer said, "you have to do it *because*
you're president of the United States."

It is the final irony—which any president will ignore at
great peril. After one particularly humiliating press dinner
in 1971, Richard Nixon composed a remarkable memo to

H. R. Haldeman. "Let me give you a hard-nosed appraisal of the White House Correspondents Dinner," he began.

> The reporters receiving the awards were way-out left wingers. . . . I had to sit there for 20 minutes while the drunken audience laughed in derision as the award citations were read. I'm not a bit thin-skinned [*sic!*], but I do have the responsibility to protect the office of the Presidency from such insulting incidents. I'm sure that [White House staffers] approved this charade because it would demonstrate that the President was a "good sport." I don't have to demonstrate that. . . . Under absolutely no circumstances will I attend any more dinners of this type in the future.

With a single exception two years later, Nixon kept his vow. And look what happened to him.

Newt Gingrich's
Opening Day

February 1995

WITH THE REPUBLICAN OCCUPATION OF
Capitol Hill, the language of politics has been sucker-punched
by paradox, poleaxed by non sequiturs: A cadre of reactionary revolutionaries, led by a conservative futurist, lays waste
to an old order of the Left with an agenda of right-wing reform.
These words are not supposed to go together; the tongue stalls,
the mind reels. This is going to take some getting used to.

But how did it happen? How could Republicans—the
party of Dad, of golf, of dark blue suits—overtake the party
of Bruce Springsteen to become the hipsters of political
change? Never underestimate the power of vocabulary. Newt
Gingrich spits out phrases like "the failed old order" as if he
were slapping down a royal flush in a game of five-card stud.
Dick Gephardt and David Bonior drone on—still!—about
the "rich" and "Wall Street," epithets circa 1933.

This sudden turnabout hits the Democrats where they live.
For the first time in fifty years, they're behind the curve.
Gingrich and his colleagues have mastered the latest dance
craze, slamming in the mosh pit to the hottest CDs. Meta-
phorically, anyway. And poor Gephardt and Bonior? They're
off in the corner, in baggy lime-green leisure suits with lemon-
yellow piping, fussing with the eight-track and trying to learn
the Hustle. If you can imagine.

But Democrats, take heart! All is not lost! You still have Lee Greenwood to kick around.

"Republicans will never be a Majority party until they figure out about music," a Republican friend said to me. It is one of the few sour notes I heard struck on January 4, the day the Republicans took over Capitol Hill. We were at the Ramada Renaissance Hotel, where thousands had paid $25 to gather for "free" dessert and a very expensive cash bar in yet another "Tribute to Newt." Only a Republican could wash down a gooey Napoleon with a tumbler of back-rail Scotch.

But my friend had put her finger on the unnerving thing. Their choice of celebratory music continues to cripple Republicans' efforts at hipness. The last great GOP celebration, President Bush's inaugural in 1989, featured the Beach Boys and Up With People—the kind of acts that middle-aged Republicans are sure "the kids" will go wild over. The Clintonites trumped this misbegotten move by reuniting Fleetwood Mac. Now, two years later, the Republicans have disinterred Lee Greenwood.

He appeared in the Renaissance ballroom in a kaleidoscope of colored lights. Strutting across the stage dressed in black, his band thumping behind him, Greenwood favors the country-outlaw couture of the early eighties, popularized by Waylon Jennings, Willie Nelson, and other people you never hear of anymore. His look offered a stark contrast to his audience of well-coiffed Washingtonians; he looked like he'd just washed his hair in a crank case. The music grew louder from song to song. When Greenwood hit the final chorus of "Georgia on My Mind," the crowd fairly swooned. At once the house lights flashed on, and Gingrich himself appeared onstage, rock-star fashion, to volcanic applause. It was a strange discontinuity between buildup and payoff, foreplay and climax, as if Mr. Rogers decided to open his TV show with the *1812 Overture*.

* * *

Gingrich, of course, does not deal in kid stuff, and neither, any longer, do Republicans. Well, not often. "Let me tell you," Gingrich told the audience, "from the standpoint of the classic liberal Democratic vision of the old, stuffy, country-club Republican party . . . this isn't it!" A roar rose from the crowd, most of whom at that very moment could have been airdropped onto the veranda at the Chevy Chase Club without raising an eyebrow, or spilling a drop of gin-and-tonic.

But then something untoward happened. Gingrich mentioned that the "liberal press corps" shared in this outmoded vision of the Republicans, and the Grand Old Partygoers turned as one to the press pen at the side of the ballroom, chanting "Newt!" and thrusting index fingers at the hapless reporters and cameramen. Most of us reporters began scribbling very fast in our notebooks. Over the din, one asked: "Do you think we'll get out of here alive?" He was only half joking.

This silly antipathy, unchecked, will hobble the new regime even more than its unfortunate taste in musical entertainment. The resentment betrays an insecurity unbecoming a revolution. Before Gingrich's press conference on opening day, reporters lined up outside the Capitol's Rayburn Room, where the press conference was to be held. Tourists, most wearing "Happy Newt Year" or "Friend of Newt" buttons, streamed past. When one of the Newtonians overheard a reporter's comment about "fat cats," he stopped cold. "You arrogant bastards!" he shouted, with a sweep of his arm. Before waddling on (he was not, in truth, a thin cat), he hissed: *"Sic semper tyrannis!"*

Alas, the feeling is mutual. Farther back in line, two well-known newspaper columnists matter-of-factly discussed the new Speaker. "Tell me," one asked the other, "what do you suppose is the most despicable thing he's ever done? That we know about, I mean."

"Tough question," said her colleague.

Just a couple of newsmen, comparing notes. Shop talk.

The rancor of this revolution moves in so many directions! Press v. Gingrich. Congress v. The President. Newtonians v. Press. Democrats v. Republicans. But in his opening address to the House, Gingrich tried to slather conciliation like frosting on a sweet roll. He praised the New Deal and FDR; he praised Ron Dellums and John Dingell; he praised Dick Gephardt—though he praised them as a eulogist, in order to bury them. Even in his more casual remarks he co-opted the tone of his political adversaries.

Late in the afternoon he appeared at a children's party to introduce the Mighty Morphin Power Rangers—perhaps the most disorienting what's-wrong-with-this-picture moment of the day. Given Gingrich's professorial fondness for Big Ideas, what could he have said? "Kids, in Zordon's relationship with the Power Rangers we see an extraordinary exemplification of Peter Drucker's model of the bottom-up organizational dynamic. . . ."

What he did say was startling enough. "We wanted the Power Rangers here," he told the puzzled children, "because they're multiethnic role models in which women and men play equally strong roles." Joycelyn Elders couldn't have put it better.

None of the sweet talk did any good, of course, for when the gavel came down in the House chamber, the subterranean tensions boiled to the surface. Republicans rotated in the Speaker's chair, delighting in their power to shut up their colleagues. "The gentleman's time has expired!" the chair would shout, and the gavel would fall like a guillotine. Even the deadening effects of parliamentary procedure—members scrambling to vote on the motion to table the resolution to recommit the amendment to the previous question, and what was the question again?—failed to dampen the ill feeling, and in time it grew tiresome. Before long, I sought refuge in the Senate gallery, on the other side of the Capitol.

Here, even on the first day of the Revolution, was the comity on which the world's greatest deliberative body prides itself. The pace was almost lethargic; the chamber was so quiet you could hear the air conditioning hum. Senators milled about on the blue-and-gold carpeting.

Near a paneled doorway, Chris Dodd picked lint from Al D'Amato's lapel. Teddy Kennedy, whose fresh-salmon complexion has recently subsided to a reassuring ashen pink, whispered in Pat Leahy's ear and then moved quickly out the door in an impressive imitation of Donald Duck. John Warner glided from senator to senator, delighting in the camaraderie of men who don't care that his ex-wife ran off with a construction worker named Larry Fortensky.

The most touching moment came during the swearing-in of the Senate's new president pro tempore, Strom Thurmond. Thurmond had asked that Robert Byrd escort him to the chair, as a sentimental gesture, and the traditions of collegiality were never more touching: These two old warriors, stooped with age but their dignity unbowed, walked arm in arm to the podium, as they might have done years ago as Grand Kleagles at a KKK rally.

This is the collegiality that Washington loves, that the establishment has grown used to. Catch it while you can, for the revolution of paradox and non sequiturs proceeds. Returning to the House chamber, I ran into Sonny Bono, celebrated freshman from California. I asked to interview him, out of journalistic duty, and his thoughts are worth pondering. He spoke of his own situation, which serves as a metaphor for the transformation now taking place in our political culture. I think.

"Show business and politics," he said, "they're a lot alike. People are here because it's a power game, it's an ego game. And when there's a big change coming, it humbles you.

"It's like, there are those moments in life where there's a crack that occurs in a lifetime, and you just have to kind of stand back and go, 'Whoa.' That's what's going on now."

Whoa. It is a word we will hear often in the months to come.

Tom
Foolery

A Very
Unimportant Person

April 1995

A FEW WEEKS AGO I FOUND MYSELF TAGGING
along with an earth-moving VIP as he went about his daily
duties. He was busy. It is his business to be busy. We went
from meeting to meeting, ducked in at social gatherings,
greeted countless strangers, ate on the run. Late in the
evening, however, there was a momentary lull in his schedule. He took me into a conference room and pointed to a
telephone.

"We've been running around so much, you'll probably
need some phone time," he said. He picked up another phone
and began dialing. I understood at once that I was supposed
to do the same—to fill these precious, unbusy minutes allot-
ted to us by making urgent phone calls. The problem was, I
didn't have anyone to call. It was 10:30 at night. I called my
wife.

"Everything's going fine," I told her, nodding and smiling
to the VIP across the room. He seemed happy I was making
efficient use of phone time.

"Good," said my wife.

"So I'll be home sometime later," I said.

"Great," she said.

"So."

"So," she said.

147

"I guess I'll talk to you later."

"Good," she said.

I rang off and shifted in my seat. The VIP spoke into the phone in hushed tones, hung up, dialed again, resumed speaking in hushed tones. He repeated the pattern for several minutes, while I stared at my phone. He glanced my way only occasionally, with a puzzled look, as though I had taken off my pants. And I did feel naked, in a way. Before this extraordinarily powerful man I sat exposed as a VUP, a very unimportant person, a loser—a guy who, granted the privilege of phone time, couldn't hack it. Eventually I picked up the phone again and called my office, listening to my voice-mail greeting over and over. "That's good," I said at irregular intervals, in hushed tones.

Over the next few days my feelings of inadequacy hardened into indignation, and a warm sense of superiority returned. I'm proud to be unmoved by this thoroughly modern need to be in constant touch. The ultimate trophy is the fax machine that some communication addicts are said to have in their cars; but the more commonplace cellular phone will do just as well. You see the guys and gals walking down the boulevards of every major city, these yuppies with the portable phones attached to their ears, stopping traffic, tripping over hydrants, bumping into lampposts. There are twenty-five million cellular-phone users in the United States today, displaying (I've decided) an infantile yearning for incessant stimulation, a pathetic play for self-validation, a quest for identity in quicksand: I talk on the phone, therefore I am.

I'm not sure what the point of it all is—and I wonder, sometimes, whether the communication addicts know, either. And cellular phones are just the beginning. Last summer, I signed up with an online computer service to enjoy at last the benefits of e-mail. Instant communication with anyone, anytime, anywhere in the world! To inaugurate my new life online, I e-mailed a friend in California who had been cajoling me for months to join him in cyberspace. "I'm finally online!!!" I e-mailed. (E-mail is a blunt, vigorous medium, demanding overuse of exclamation points.) I waited for his reply. After three weeks I called him. "Oh," he said, "I haven't checked my mail for a while. Let me read it." Ten minutes later he called back. "It's about time you got online," he said. "These are the nineties. How are the kids?" We had a nice long chat.

You don't have to be a latter-day Henry David Thoreau—and who would want to be?—to note the central irony of the Information Age: As our means of communication accelerate, there are fewer things of interest to talk about and fewer interesting people to talk about them with. Anyone who doubts this need only sign on to one of the "chat rooms" offered by CompuServe or America Online. "Megadeth rules!" one communicator will argue. "Megadeth sucks!" another will counter, and thus the conversation will develop, for hours and hours. So little to say, so many ways to say it. See the businessman on the transatlantic flight, with $4,000 of microcosmic hardware resting in his lap, plugging in his fax modem with trembling fingers so he can access . . . at the speed of light! in maxicolor liquid crystal display! . . . the *New York Times* op-ed page.

Oh, but why? One of the attractions of flight used to be the blessed isolation it offered. Now, with a few keystrokes, you can put Anthony Lewis in the seat next to you. I do not think this is progress. Even the most incidental moments of isolation can be avoided—thanks to the fax in the car, the portable phone in the pocket, the modem in the airplane. I'm having none of it. I embrace my VUPness with honor and pride. Like the fruitcake Thoreau, I move through life unencumbered by gadgets, unfettered by the hardware of a heedless age. Unless, of course, someone wants to buy me one of those little handheld portable TVs. (They come with color screens now.)

Gorbachev and
the Global Brain Trust

September 1995

SINCE THE END OF THE COLD WAR . . . IS ANY
opening sentence dreaded more by readers of newspapers,
magazines, and journals of opinion? *After the fall of the Berlin
Wall . . .* Synapses freeze, eyes glaze, brain cells die one by
one. *Where do we find ourselves six years after the breakup
of the Soviet empire?*

Well, here is where some of us find ourselves, this Wednes-
day evening in late September: in the Grand Ballroom of San
Francisco's Fairmont Hotel, at the kickoff dinner of the State
of the World Forum. It is a distinguished company, including
retired diplomats (George Shultz and Zbigniew Brzezinski),
Nobel laureates (Guatemala's Rigoberta Menchu and the Bell
Labs physicist Arno Penzias), science popularizers (Carl
Sagan and Fritjof Capra), movie stars (Jane Fonda and
Shirley MacLaine), rich guys (Ted Turner and David
Packard), New Age gurus (Sam Keen and Deepak Chopra),
and many more—five hundred in all, leading lights from
business, politics, religion, and the arts. Such an extraordinary collection of talent, of human knowledge and spiritual
insight, has not been seen in a single room since Bill Moyers
dined alone.

And at the dais, making welcoming remarks through an
interpreter, is Mikhail Gorbachev. With his forum cochairman,

James Garrison, Gorbachev has hand-picked the invitees, most of whom have paid $5,000 to attend. It is now almost 11 P.M. Dinner has been served, the plates cleared away, and little candles cast sleepy pools of light across the crystal, showing the lipstick smudges and fingerprints made greasy from the beef medallions in shashlik marinade.

Gorbachev has been talking for twenty-five minutes, in low tones followed by the high-pitched, stuttering translation of his interpreter. He is still pointing out people in the audience. Here's his good friend George Mitchell, and over there is his even better friend Alan Cranston. Five more minutes pass. In the dark the seated figures begin to fidget. And here is Thabo Mbeki, deputy president of South Africa, another good friend. Jane Fonda, head lowered, squats out of her seat, does a duck walk to the exit. At length Gorbachev seems to be winding down. The audience leans forward, poised for an ovation and hasty retreat. Gorbachev takes a breath. "And now," he says, "my colleagues have suggested I give a broad overview of our current world situation."

And over the vast ballroom the realization presses down like a damp blanket: *He's just getting started.*

Yet no one dares follow Fonda to the exit. For another half hour or longer he goes on, displaying a public-speaking technique refined over years of addressing iron-butted apparatchiks in endless Central Committee meetings. Bromide falls upon bromide. "There are profound layers among the interfaces of politics, geopolitics, and philosophy," he says. Will he list them all? In the general catalepsy no one stirs.

And one can't help but wonder, there in the dark: Why not? What mysterious centrifugal force, beyond politeness, keeps the forum-goers in their seats? What impels Gorbachev to drone on, and his listeners to listen, here in a grand hotel, six years after the breakup of the Soviet empire?

Over the next four days Mikhail Gorbachev, along with Sam Keen and Ted Turner and Deepak Chopra and the rest, make the answer plain: They are busy creating a New Civilization—for all of us. And a little boredom is a small price to pay.

"This is the first step in establishing a global brain trust," Gorbachev said that night, and the New Civilization is its top priority. This was merely the *first* State of the World Forum. The brain trust plans to meet at least once a year through 2000, with Gorbachev as convener. In the four years since he felt the boot of the Russian people, he has gathered the experience necessary to serve as the brain trust's nucleus. He travels the world these days as an international sage, attending forums on the Twenty-first Century, the Future of Democracy, Democracy in the Twenty-first Century, the Democracy of the Future, the Future of the Twenty-first Century, and other stately themes. A global infrastructure of foundations, philanthropists, corporate interests, and academic institutions sustains him and picks up the tab.

It is a good life, as he says himself: "I have many things to keep me busy." One of those is the Gorbachev Foundation, which he cofounded with Garrison in San Francisco and Moscow and which sponsored the State of the World Forum. Another is the International Green Cross, of which he is president. Having led the most environmentally profligate empire in history, Gorby in retirement has gone green. Apocalyptic environmentalism is the creed that undergirds the global brain trust. "A new civilization would mean, above all, solving the problems that exist between man and the rest of nature," he told *Audubon* magazine last year. "If these problems are not solved, the rest is nonsense."

For Gorbachev and his fellow brain trusters, environmentalism satisfies several needs at once. It is quasi-religious, allowing for talk of values and "the spiritual." "A revolution has to take place in people's minds," he likes to say. For its adherents and even its distant sympathizers, the implosion of communism left a void; ecological alarmism fills it, for like communism it is a unified field theory of social organization. And just as important, environmentalism encourages Gorbachev and his colleagues to sustain the moral equivalence that was their chief rhetorical safeguard during the Cold War. The "global ecological crisis" proves that capitalism as well as communism has failed. "Now that we are rid of this syndrome of imposing the communist model on people," he told *Audubon*, "I have to tell you Americans that you've been pushing your American way of life for decades. There has to be a different approach. Americans have to be more modest in their desires."

Perhaps most important of all, environmentalism allows Gorbachev to speak in just such big, blowy tropes. He has mastered the alarmist platitude. He is a global Polonius. "There is a sweeping crisis that threatens our civilization," Gorbachev told the forum, more than once. "The most profound need is to move away from a technology-centered to a culture-centered way of living. We must change the nature of consumption so that it is geared toward our cultural needs. With the growing scarcity of resources, we must focus on the need to control the global process."

For years, commentators speculated on Gorbachev's intellectual development, as he worked his way through the classics of Western political thought: from Aristotle to the Declaration of Independence and the Federalist Papers, through Lincoln and even to Hayek. He has finally come to rest, on the *Whole Earth Catalog*.

Gorbachev's global brain trust relishes its variety, drawn as it is, self-consciously, from the fields of business and religion, science and politics. Participants were brought to the Fairmont for a series of plenary sessions and roundtable discussions. The themes were Gorbachevian—New Indicators for Measuring Sustainable Development; Facing the Planet's

Carrying Capacity; Ecology: The New Science of the Sacred;
and many others. As these grand themes were chewed over,
the variety of the participants' backgrounds was meant to
result in unexpected synergies of insight.

On close inspection, however, the variety of the brain trust
looks less various. David Packard and Ted Turner notwithstanding, the businessfolk tend to airy job descriptions—
"specialists in international empowerment strategies" and
"consultants" in such corporate shakedown rackets as
"environmental performance" and "disability compliance."
The politicians are all out of work: Brian Mulroney, Jim
Sasser, Gorbachev himself. Most of the scientists labor in
"New Science"; Rupert Sheldrake, for example, though once
a biochemist at Cambridge, has spent the last several years
working on a "morphic field theory of the mind," which aims
to prove that the "sun is thinking." "Religious leaders" are
almost exclusively Buddhist, Vedantist, or Shirley MacLaine.
The rest of the participants were drawn from what they call
"civic society," a euphemism for nonprofits. Peggy Dulany,
to cite one case, is spending her legacy as a Rockefeller scion
on squatter camps in Latin America. Michael Murphy, the
founder of the Esalen Institute, has been investigating the
mystical experiences of golfers.

Among those in the brain trust, however, there is still room
for paradox, if not friction. Early Thursday morning, at the
start of the first plenary session, I sat in the press pen, listening to keynoter Thabo Mbeki, the former South African ANC
activist and now Nelson Mandela's number two. He deplored,
gently, the sparse African presence at the forum, insinuating
that there might be a First World bias at work. At that
moment, Ted Turner plopped down next to me, seeming agi-
tated. Turner tore open his copy of the day's *New York Times*
and turned at once to the Business page. A banner headline
read: "Turner Pay Deal Said to Top $100 million."

"Will the poor of the world be able to participate in our agenda?" Mbeki asked from the podium.

Turner read with furrowed brow, his finger tracing down the page: "As the new vice chairman of Time Warner, Mr. Turner is to receive a five-year compensation package worth well in excess of $100 million.

"Will they have a say in the growing gap of wealth in the world?" Mbeki wondered.

Turner kept reading: "Add that to the $75 million in salary, bonus and long-term compensation. . ."

"Will they continue to be left behind in the communication revolution?" Mbeki said. His voice rose, but Ted didn't appear to be listening.

The nettlesome contrast recurred. The corn-producer Archer-Daniels-Midland underwrote the forum for $250,000. No company is so intent that the Third World achieve "sustainable development." And not a penny more than *sustainable*—surely not to the point where those countries start exporting corn.

ADM is a conservative entity that feints left; among the brain trust, the process more often runs in the other direction. Garrison, Gorbachev's cochair and the man who brought the brain trust into being, declined to be interviewed at the forum. But a recent profile in *SF Weekly* revealed his career to be a kind of synecdoche for the American Left and its evolution over the last twenty years. In miniature, it is the story of the brain trust itself.

Garrison is a slight man, short as Gorbachev and half as heavy. His tailored suits hang straight down from his shoulders. Though forty-four, he looks a few months shy of getting his driver's license. He has the quiet air of a divinity student, which he once was. He studied at Harvard, then at Cambridge, where he earned a Ph.D. under the radical theologian J. A. T. Robinson. In the mid-seventies he became active in

156

ANDREW FERGUSON

the antinuclear movement, chaining himself to bulldozers outside midwestern power plants. He later fused his spiritual interests with his activism by helping to found the Christic Institute. The Institute gained notoriety as the chief publicist for the "Secret Team" conspiracy theory, which characterized the Cold War as a fraud imposed upon a peace-loving planet by a shadowy team of American intelligence officers.

Slowly, as the Left eroded under the Reagan Terror, Garrison felt the tug of commerce. Throughout the eighties, as a freelance peacenik, he traveled often to the Soviet Union and established contacts within the Politburo. His Rolodex swelled. "I could leverage my contacts to meet a Kissinger or a George Shultz," he told *SF Weekly*. "I became important because I could deliver important Soviets." When communism collapsed, he parlayed his network of friendships into investment opportunities. He organized U.S. speaking tours for Gorbachev, Eduard Shevardnadze, and Boris Yeltsin. His investment-consulting firm, based in San Francisco, flourished with deals in the former Soviet bloc. In the mainstream at last, he even ran for Congress and is now said to be eyeing a Senate race. Today he is a very wealthy man, perhaps the only operator in the world who's on a first-name basis with both George Shultz and the New Age healer Deepak Chopra—an embodiment of the New New Left.

He is also enormously competent, a virtue seldom associated with people who chain themselves to bulldozers. The forum was a massive logistical enterprise, and it operated with the elegant precision of a Swiss railroad. Staffers with walkie-talkies and earpieces quietly guided participants from event to event. Sessions never ran overtime, unless Gorbachev wanted to say something. Meals were prepared by celebrity chefs, including Wolfgang Puck, and diners were serenaded by New Age musicians gently playing their dulcimers and tablas and bells.

For the American Left, the introduction of New Age spirituality is the most significant development since the trial of
the Scottsboro Boys—or at least since the divorce of Jane
Fonda and Tom Hayden. (It is always "spirituality," by the
way, never "religion"; and never, God forbid, "God.") A
Vietnamese monk was on hand to instruct participants in
meditation techniques. Drawing on his huge bestseller, *Ageless Body, Timeless Mind*, Deepak Chopra spoke in one room
of the seven levels of consciousness, while New Economists
outlined the Love Economy in the room next door. Gorbachev
himself spoke freely of "transforming human consciousness."
In the press room, reporters from *Earth Times* and *Disarma-
ment News* did yogic stretching exercises, emitting little moans.
A makeshift bookstore sold CDs like "Sacred Healing Chants
of Tibet" and "Exploring the Cosmic Christ" and books like
Jesus, CEO: Using Ancient Wisdom for Visionary Leadership.

Aside from Garrison himself, no one understands this final,
decadent phase of the Left better than Danny Sheehan, a
well-known political activist who, like Garrison, was one of
the founders of the Christic Institute. On the last day of the
forum, I buttonholed him outside the Grand Ballroom.

"A couple of things can come from this forum," he said, in
his breathless manner. "Like I was in the bathroom just now.
And I saw Ruud Lubbers [the former prime minister of the
Netherlands]. I was on a panel with him—and just now I called
him 'Ruud.' He calls Gorbachev 'Michael.'" First names. So
there's a friendship thing happening. The statespersons get
to be friends with the New Scientists who get to be friends
with the spiritual leaders who get to be friends with the statespersons. This is potentially paradigm-impacting.

"Since the end of the Cold War, we have a brief window
here where we can undo all the old paradigms. You know
there's the old Newtonian, Cartesian paradigm—units of
matter colliding in space like Ping-Pong balls. All our present
institutions are based on that rationalist model. But we've

known since Heisenberg and the uncertainty principle that this paradigm isn't true. It's not accurate. There are no ultimate integers of matter, just networks of potentialities. Everything is ultimately related to everything else. No absolutes.

"So what we're saying is: We must build our public policy-making institutions on this new view of what reality is."

I said, "Wow. Is Gorbachev on board with this?"

"I've spent enough time with him to know that he has a genuine insight into the spiritual dimension. He's not comfortable talking about it. But he's very into it."

All of which could sound sort of scary, until you actually watch our new global brain trust in action, or nonaction. Its main product is talk—working papers and action plans, emphasis on the *papers* and *plans*. Still, the great unanswered question of the forum was the practical one: How to impose this new view of reality, how to create a New Civilization?

I left Sheehan and walked into the final plenary session. The next morning Gorbachev would host his friends George Bush and Margaret Thatcher, neither of whom attended the forum proper, for an hour-long roundtable broadcast by CNN. But this plenary on Saturday afternoon was to be the official summing-up.

The ballroom was packed. Each roundtable discussion group had a leader, and one by one they made their way to the dais to present their findings to Gorbachev and the assembled brain trust. Alan Cranston, once a U.S. senator from California, went first. Over the previous four days he had led a group in discussing "The New Architecture of Global Security." Under the pitiless stage lights he looked like a woodcut by Edvard Munch. His roundtable had produced eminently practical suggestions, he said. A ban on nuclear testing. Enlargement of the U.N. Security Council. And allowing people to vote for their country's U.N. representative. He finished to polite applause.

Then came Sam Keen, the men's movement maven who was discovered by Bill Moyers. His roundtable had discussed "The Global Crisis of the Spirit." The solutions to the crisis: "A re-enchantment of the world." "Stopping the colonization of the spirit by commercial interests." And one other idea: "If we cut the world's population by 90 percent, there won't be enough people left to do ecological damage." The ovation shook the chandeliers.

And so it went. At last Stephen Rhinesmith—identified as a "specialist on global business strategy implementation"— rose to close the session. "For four days," he said, "we have lived together, talked together, hoped together." In the ballroom, several brain trusters held hands. There was silence. Rhinesmith offered "four action steps—things we can all do as we move from this place." They were: 1) Think of what it all means to you. 2) Think about what we can do as a community. 3) Think about what "we can do as representatives of the people we represent." And 4) Think of what we can do as participants in the global community.

None of these, of course, is really "a thing to do," and from this fact the rest of us can take comfort. Imagine the problems the global brain trust would present for the world if it had stormed from the Fairmont agitating to nationalize the banks or institute mandatory bedtime. That, or something similar, would have been the agenda a mere decade ago, before the fall of the Wall, when the Left was in full flower. But for now the brain trusters seem content merely to interface among themselves.

After the thunderous applause for Rhinesmith, people got up to go. Gorbachev, godfather of the New Civilization, seized the microphone. "I have a two-minute comment," he said. I left the ballroom twenty minutes later. He was still talking.

Chasing Rainbows

January 1994

IS ALLEN FUNT DEAD? I'D FEEL A LOT BETTER if he were. Life in America these days seems like an endless string of scenarios designed to make you—or some of us, anyway—feel out of it, clueless, not with the program, a *chump*. And sometimes, just when you're starting to get in the swing of things, not wanting to be a jerk, you half expect a door to swing open to reveal the creator of *Candid Camera*, hollering "Smile!" and proving—just when you least expect it!—that you are, indeed, a chump.

Consider, for example, a cold January morning in a hallway of the Omni Shoreham Hotel in Washington, D.C. A man who calls himself a "facilitator" tells me we are on a bus, although I'm very sure that we're standing in a hallway. He says the bus is coming from "Alphaland." He hands me several cards of various colors and sends me into a conference room, which he calls "Betaland." I am at once surrounded by people I barely know. Each of them is also holding cards. "Bafa ba!" bellows an administrator from a local school system.

"Wo? Wo!!" shouts a personnel director from a midwestern corporation.

A high school teacher crowds in on me, touches his chin to his chest, and then grabs one of my cards and says, with some heat, "Ro, ro."

A consultant from Denver, taking pity, pulls me aside. "Yo, wo, ro," she says, pushing her cards into my face. "Ba fa ba."

Presently the facilitator comes to take me away, in our little nonexistent bus. In a few minutes we are all reunited again in the conference room.

"Let's talk," says the facilitator. "How did you experience this?"

"I felt fear," says a consultant from Montgomery County. "I felt anger. I felt very alone."

I search the faces around the room. Not a smile, not a wry twinkle, not a flicker of irony.

"Thank you," says the facilitator, much moved. "Thank you for that." In the silence everyone nods grimly. Everyone, that is, but me, who pulls back, and wonders.

Allen? Mr. Funt? Are you there?

The Shoreham on that cold morning was playing host to the National MultiCultural Institute's conference "Building Personal and Cultural Competence in a Multicultural Society." It was a swirl of lectures and presentations, seminars and workshops, including the one in which I was enrolled: "Diversity 101: Developing Cultural Awareness." Each dealt with the hottest topic in American business today: "managing diversity" in the workforce, by training managers and employees to "value difference." Business's obsession with diversity has spawned an industry of its own, with a host of new professional life forms, all of whom were represented at the Shoreham: trainers, educators, personnel department personnel, consultants, counselors, human resource officials, equal opportunity overseers, conflict resolution experts, group dynamics theorists, affirmative action directors, equal employment opportunity compliance officers, and organizational development specialists.

If you think the job titles are ambiguous, the subject that has brought them together is fuzzier still. Diversity training,

according to NMCI, teaches us "to work with a diverse group
of people in a manner that enables them to reach their full
potential in pursuit of organizational objectives, without anyone being advantaged or disadvantaged by irrelevant con-
siderations." According to another trainer, it's "going deep
inside yourself to confront the biases that we have." Still
another trainer says, "It's not just about understanding, it's
about changing who you are." In fact, diversity training is
much more than that, and much less. What it really is, is a
gold mine.

Ten years ago nobody called himself a "diversity trainer."
Today, there are as many as five thousand nationwide, with
more hanging out their shingles daily; almost all large management consulting firms employ people who specialize in
diversity. The trainers—or facilitators, as they also are
known—trace the origins of their profession to 1987, when
a think tank called the Hudson Institute released a widely
publicized report, "Workforce 2000." The report predicted
that by the end of the century, only 15 percent of the people
entering the workforce would be native-born white males.

This was taken as a firebell in the night by many native-
born white-male businessmen: It happened to General Custer,
it can happen to us! Accordingly, most Fortune 500 companies have undertaken diversity training for their senior managers and hefty segments of their workforce. In Washington,
the area's largest employers—local utilities, private corporations like MCI and Marriott, county and state governments,
an alphabet soup of federal agencies from the FBI to the NRC
to DOT—have done likewise. The format differs from company to company, but most often diversity training entails
gathering employees and managers into small groups for
sessions ranging from two hours to three days. Sometimes
the training is voluntary, but it is always "strongly encouraged" by the boss. The trainees hear lectures and watch videos
on cultural diversity, play games to heighten their "cultural

awareness," do "experiential exercises" to sensitize them to the feelings of others, and then "dialogue" and "process information" in group discussions.

All of which costs companies a great deal of money. Nevertheless, the demand for diversity training outstrips supply; trainers are routinely booked months in advance. They earn at a minimum $1,500 to $2,000 a day; a medium-sized workforce could take a month or more to train. Long-range contracts of $500,000 a year are common.

It's nice work if you can get it. And even better: Almost anyone can get it. There is no certification, by a national board or any other mechanism, to qualify diversity trainers—no tests to study for, no oral exams to fidget through, no dissertations to prove your expertise. To become a trainer you have only to call yourself one and hope that a network of friends, colleagues, and potential clients spreads the word of your new self-designation. A degree in one of the softer sciences—education, sociology, organizational development—is nice but not essential. (Interestingly, few trainers have a background in business, though this seems not to bother the businessmen who hire them.) Nor is a large capital outlay required to set up shop. A number of mail-order houses offer packages of "diversity materials": workbooks and worksheets ($99.95 and up), boardgames ($75 and up), transparencies for overhead projectors ($12). Videos—a requirement for every trainer's kitbag—do cost more: for example, "Competing Through Managing Diversity," a new two-part video by the mahatma of diversity training, R. Roosevelt Thomas of Morehouse College in Atlanta, costs $2,000, though this includes a handsome workbook printed on lush paper. Even so, a fully outfitted diversity trainer can be in the black after his first day's work.

"I lecture at colleges and universities," says Dr. Lennox Joseph, a management consultant in Alexandria, "and students will often ask me how to get started in consulting. I tell them, 'If you want to make a large amount of money in a very short period of time, go into diversity.'"

So you have your workbook and worksheets, your videos and transparencies, a boardgame or two: you are perforce a diversity consultant, no? That depends. Every diversity consultant must have something else, internalized until it's almost second nature: the dogma of diversity—a closed system of business jargon, left-wing politics, and the techniques of the "human potential movement," packaged to attract corporate managers obsessed with the bottom line. To understand why diversity training has gripped American business, you must understand this strange coagulation of forces— politics, business, and the enthusiasms of popular psychology.

Diversity training is a purely American phenomenon; it is impossible to imagine the French, say, or the Spanish, much less the Serbs, devoting vast amounts of business income to such an endeavor. But among the world's peoples, the American businessman is also unique. He has created the most prosperous society in history, owing largely to his remarkable openness to new ideas—which is a kind way of saying he will fall for almost anything, so long as it is dressed up as a boon to commerce.

A quick scan of the business bookshelf at the local B. Dalton or Crown Books testifies to the fact. There, gleaming in rows like plumped polished fruit, you'll find the successors to Dale Carnegie's *How to Win Friends and Influence People* and Napoleon Hill's *Think and Grow Rich*. Like their legendary forebears, the newer books are put together according to a method of elegant simplicity. A platitude, any platitude—let's say: a successful manager is one who is sensitive to new and unexpected competitive pressures—is teased into two hundred pages of anecdotes, pie charts, tables, and bold-faced type. A catch phrase, preferably including the words "leadership" and "management," is attached as a title. Thus: *The*

West Point Way of Leadership, Enlightened Leadership, Liberation Management, Total Behavior Management, Managing Quality, Total Quality Leadership, and even *Management Tips from Red Auerbach.* (Red Auerbach!)

For the Babbitt of late-twentieth-century America, these books can hold an almost talismanic power. Within them, in cold black and white, buried among the buzzword prose and the dubious diagrams, is the secret of *making it:* creating the corporation of the next century, sleek, flexible, lean and mean, in five simple steps that turn challenge into opportunity! The books, these sacred texts, are not only bought in large numbers but read with great devotion. Walk the aisle of the Metroliner or the Delta shuttle, glance about the waiting lounges at O'Hare and Hartsfield and La Guardia, and you'll see the middle managers crack the book spine and remove the Parker rollerball from their Joseph Banks pinstripes and make little checks and exclamation points next to such sentences as: "Individuals must be helped to explore ways of facilitating mutual adaptation on the part of the individual and the organization." The charts and graphs, lending an air of scientific rigor to the mysticism, get copied into the back pages of Filofaxes. The brow furrows, the tongue slides through pursed lips: the five steps are memorized, the secret is passed on!

What shall we call this weakness of the American businessman? Suggestibility? Gullibility? Whatever: inevitably it joined itself to another purely American phenomenon, the human potential movement, also known, more recently, as the New Age. At first, of course, encounter groups and est and primal therapy and transcendental meditation drew their adherents from the flotsam and jetsam of 1960s America, from runaway Radcliffe coeds and dispirited advertising account executives who had taken to wearing sandals and sideburns when the midlife crisis hit. They too were after the secret—to happiness, spiritual integration, the peak experience—and pop-psych wizards like Abraham Maslow and Fritz Perls told them it could be found by *talking*, preferably about oneself and one's feelings. Talk could "break down barriers," lift the workaday to the realm of the exotic, make little dramas out of the dingy dailiness of our lives, and what made the drama so intoxicating was that the hero was . . . me! Souls were opened up like a can of 10–40 motor oil and the innermost thoughts came sliding out, in the name of personal growth. From Esalen and Marin County and Topanga Canyon, the word went forth to America: *Let's talk!*

In time this came to be called "sharing," which lent an altruistic flavor to the thing, masking what an earlier age might have called self-indulgence, or whining. As it turned out, however, that antique notion of self-restraint continued to hold large numbers in its thrall, so facilitators devised techniques to loosen up the squares and tight asses and the occasional Babbitt: simulations and role playing and games to "break down the barriers."

And it worked! Oh lord how it worked! The talk poured out in a Niagara—and what talk it was! About my feelings and your feelings, about my feelings about your feelings about me and what Dad did to me when Mom wasn't looking, and no secret was too dark, too private to be shared. Communication was therapy, and no problem could survive its ministrations. A refusal to share, even after all the simulations and role playing, could only be a symptom of pathology, usually called denial; reticence replaced sin; therapy became salvation.

To a Protestant country unfamiliar with the rite of confession, the value of talk came as a revelation. The human potential movement swept out from California and saturated the country's public life. Before long, Methodist and Lutheran churches were holding encounter groups in their cinder-block basements. Workshops crowded the public rooms of the local library. Consciousness-raising sessions supplanted the gossipy coffee klatsch in suburban living rooms while the guys were at work. America hasn't shut up since. Sharing is epidemic, as the guests on Oprah and Sally Jessy attest. No one is immune. When President Clinton, an Adult Child of an Alcoholic, famously told a group of homosexual activists, "I feel your pain," he spoke the language of the New Age. His self-designation as a "change agent" also comes from the personal-growth lexicon. And when, in his inaugural, he beseeched us "to make change our friend," he might have lifted the sing-songy sentence from the works of Leo Buscaglia.

Shortly after the inauguration, the *Washington Post* reported that the president had invited his entire Cabinet to Camp David, where a facilitator led them in a kind of encounter group. The president himself shared with the group the interesting datum that as a boy he had been taunted for being a fat little fellow. Thirty years ago such an episode would have raised hackles, if not calls for impeachment, and indeed in some corners of the political world snickering was heard. (Tight asses!) But more telling was the silence that greeted the story everywhere else. The reason is simple: the most "conservative" elements of America, the business community, the button-down squares whose hackles should have been raised, had been doing precisely the same thing for years.

In search of new ways to bolster the bottom line, the legendary George Babbitt, cornerstone of American prosperity, paragon of self-control and self-discipline, had wandered into the New Age. From Norman Vincent Peale to Dr. Wayne Dyer, from *The Power of Positive Thinking* to *I'm OK—You're OK*—it is not so long a leap. The secret of "Dynamic Managing" and "Teamthink" was conflated with the secret of personal growth. For the business to grow, the businessman must grow. By the late 1980s, senior managers at most Fortune 500 companies were veteran workshoppers. They had been on team-building retreats where facilitators wrapped them in blindfolds and led them around on leashes. They had hit each other over the heads with foam-rubber baseball bats. They had been made to sit on one another's laps and speak the secrets of their hearts. In one popular exercise the managers passed around a roll of toilet paper—with their teeth. The consensus had been reached: The old ways of the tight ass, the Kiwanis Club Babbitt, were ill suited for profit in the New Age.

The histrionics of the New Age and the gullibility of business-men make for a powerful combination, issuing in all kinds of absurdity. But together they are not sufficient to explain diversity training. A final ingredient must be added: politics.

As the New Age swept into the corporate boardrooms, a similarly portentous evolution was taking place in the civil rights movement. Rhetorically and tactically, leaders in the battle for civil rights had from the earliest stages concentrated on specific acts of discrimination: particularly those flowing from laws and practices that denied citizens access to basic rights and services. This is the spirit that animated, for example, the Civil Rights Act of 1964 and the Voting Rights Act of 1965.

In implementation, however, a subtle but unmistakable shift took place in government antidiscrimination policy. Discrimination came to be defined not as discrete acts of malice against specific individuals, but as a historical pattern embedded in organizations in general and society at large. Racism, in this view, was structural, woven into the warp and woof of America's institutions, and, what's more, deeply embedded in the way Americans were raised. Civil lawsuits, Supreme Court rulings, and punishments meted out by the Equal Employment Opportunity Commission hammered the point home: Remedies for structural racism also had to be structural, in the form of preferential hiring for members of aggrieved groups, through goals, timetables, and informal quotas.

With this change the quest for civil rights became more hospitable to what was known as the New Left, whose indictment of American society was likewise wholesale: It was an irredeemably corrupt empire, insusceptible to the tinkerings of old-fashioned reform, that could only be transformed inside out. With the credo "The personal is political," activists of the 1960s saw political change and personal growth as not just complementary but identical. The exploitive crudities of capitalism and imperialism, of the white-male power structure, could be uprooted only by altering the exploitive and crude individual consciousness of Americans themselves. The New Left's founding document, the "Port Huron statement" of 1962, set the movement's goal as "self-cultivation, self-direction, self-understanding, and creativity." To cultivate the self—in service of the larger cause of social change—the New Lefties borrowed liberally from the human potential movement. Like their group-therapy models, radicals of the sixties and early seventies were great talkers. One memoir of the era recounts an endless meeting of the Cleveland chapter of the Students for a Democratic Society, during which the members dialogued and shared for twenty-four hours straight, trying to decide whether to go to the beach.

Of course, the New Left is history. No one any longer will admit to having been a member of it; it would be like bragging you were once a Branch Davidian. But as its foot soldiers went back to graduate school or joined law firms or opened up high-tech consulting businesses, they kept the spirit alive. And it wasn't long before they noticed that the shifting definition of discrimination, which conformed so closely to their own critiques of America, left employers in a dilemma. If discrimination is institutional—if it is not simply a matter of the barbaric behavior of one manager or employee to another—then no amount of goals and timetables and sotto voce quotas could indemnify them against the charge of discrimination.

And the mere charge of discrimination was the least of it. For where there was a charge, there was a lawsuit lurking, too, probably a class-action suit, and horrid publicity that could shrivel up your market share like a dried apricot. Between 1970 and 1989, the number of discrimination suits in federal courts rose by an astonishing 2,100 percent. Judgments routinely run into the millions. The smart employer, especially one with government contracts, is prepared to show he has gone that extra mile—not merely to make his workforce look like America, but also to change the *culture* of the company, from the inside out, or at least make people think he was changing it.

Still, this was a hard pill to swallow, even for the most tremulous businessman. Someone had to make the case that changing the culture of the business was good business sense—a boost to the bottom line. Those who would make the case had two things going for them: First, the proven gullibility of the Babbitts. And second, the worry fever that gripped America in the late 1980s, a collection of anxieties that gathered around the word "competitiveness": The economy is global! A new world is dawning! The Germans and the Japanese are catching up! America is falling behind! And sure enough the books started appearing at the local B. Dalton and then in the sweaty palms of the middle managers lounging at Hartsfield and O'Hare: *Managing a Diverse Workforce: Regaining the Competitive Edge. Workforce America: Managing Employee Diversity as a Vital Workforce. Beyond Race and Gender: Unleashing the Power of Your Total Workforce by Managing Diversity.* The authors knew the business-book format: the pages were choked with the pie charts and tables, the diagrams and "action steps," the "doer models" and "empowerment models," all the schema and windy prose and bold-faced type necessary to convince the Babbitts that the secret was being passed on.

"Managing diversity" became a catchword to rival "Total Quality" and "Teamthink" and "Maximarketing." Just as Norman Vincent Peale had promised success through the "power of positive thinking" and Napoleon Hill through "magnetizing thoughts," the new dogma of diversity insinuated itself in the business world as a method of gaining victory in the marketplace. The goal, as always, was inarguable, almost banal: a workforce that is a gorgeous mosaic, synergistic, accommodating, supernaturally productive, a rainbow Utopia uniting employees of every imaginable gender, skin color, religious affiliation, and ethnic origin in a single blissful harmony.

So we can beat hell out of the Japs.

Back at the Shoreham, on the second day of our two-day workshop, the facilitator says: "We're getting into the complexities, now."

He shoots us a meaningful glance. "I want us to be very candid about some simple, ugly facts." Most of the workshoppers lean forward. "And the fact is that this country has a despicable history of dealing with difference."

The workshoppers, a voluble crew, nod and jump right in.

"Why won't the group that has power in this country," says a human resources manager from Kansas City, "understand that there's a difference between power *with* and power *over*? Why do they have to hold on to it? Why can't they just own their prejudice and say 'I benefit every day from the disadvantage I cause other people'?"

A "logistics specialist" from Denver jumps in, too. "How is it that they find it necessary that to be advantaged, they must say 'I must disadvantage you'?"

"We're going to be fighting this fight a long time," says a state employee from Pensacola. "They won't give it up willingly, is my experience."

"It's a function of capitalism, isn't it," says the facilitator. "Capitalism requires scarcity to function. It's built into the system—no scarcity, no profit.

"That's the kind of power relationships capitalism creates. Sharing power is not something a male-dominated culture naturally gravitates towards, is it? So we must create a setting where the powerful want to make changes toward the multicultural. Sometimes force is necessary. If there aren't more who'll do this on their own, then a force situation *will* become necessary. But hey—I'm not a gloom-and-doom–type person!"

I should hope not! A man who gets capitalists to pay him $2,000 a day to talk about capitalism's exploitation of scarcity has no reason to be gloomy! And ditto his workshoppers, whose bosses have flown them into Washington to stay at a $120-a-night hotel to attend a two-day workshop for a mere $500! Check that gloom and doom with the bellhop!

The ghosts of Theodor Adorno, Herbert Marcuse, and all the other New Left deep thinkers shimmer through diversity training. While the pop books at the B. Dalton show the middle managers the smiley face of "managing diversity," groups like the National MultiCultural Institute deal in the hard-core stuff, training trainers themselves in the theoretical underpinning of "managing diversity."

The literature offered by the institute lays out the diversity dogma in detail. It starts with the pleasant assumption bequeathed to us by Jean Jacques Rousseau: No one is born bad. Then society takes over, according to the literature, and "through a painful process of social conditioning" introduces the evils of "racism, classism, adultism, anti-Semitism, heterosexism," etc. "In this society we have all experienced systematic mistreatment as young people." And look what that has wrought! "Racism is one subsystem of a pervasive system of domination which presently manifests itself in many forms in American society. Sexism and ageism are examples of other subsystems. These many forms of domination constantly interact with and reinforce each other."

The invocation of "society" as all-purpose demon—a kind of stock villain like Oilcan Harry, who tied the heroine to the railroad tracks in countless silent movies—is absolutely essential. "Our parents, friends, etc., did not intend to feed us misinformation. They were simply passing on to us whatever messages had been handed down to them," which were in turn passed on to *them*, and so on. Blaming "society" stops what could be an infinite regression and allows us to disperse culpability for the horror of American culture. If society is to blame, then we all, as members of society, are to blame; and, conversely, since society is to blame, no one is to blame.

These patterns of racism, ageism, and the rest become "mental tapes"—another term borrowed from the human potential movement. "Most of us are still on automatic," says the NMCI literature. But there is a way to erase the tapes—through diversity training. "Anti-racism work is consciousness-changing work," the literature goes on. "It involves not only changing attitudes and behaviors, but also the way we see reality, the way we understand what it means to be a person . . . redefining our relationship with power and understanding on a deep level our interdependence with all life . . . with our minds, our bodies, our hearts, our spirit, with a balance of attention inward and outward."

The way we see reality! Consciousness-changing! The poor Babbitt has a right to wonder: What the hell? All he wanted was to goose the bottom line!

Well, what do you expect for $2,000 a day? The institute's literature goes on to tell the trainer what to watch for as he (or she!) herds his sheep through consciousness changing. Of particular concern are "majority members," defined as "1) European Americans, 2) Men, 3) Heterosexuals, 4) Non-handicapped people," etc. Babbitts, to sum up.

At the first stage, the "Contact Stage," the majority member is deeply deluded, "in denial," to use the terminology. He "tends to assume that racist and cultural differences are unimportant." He "believes that everyone is the same"; he "believes in the melting pot theory of assimilation." And he says things like: "When I talk to you, I don't think of you as black."

Just wait, Babbitt! Before long, if the training goes according to plan, he will progress to Stage 2, the "Disintegration Stage," in which "guilt may emerge." (Delicious!) Now he "wants to be seen as an individual and not a member of any group" and says things like: "I am not like most men, I am very sensitive to the needs of women."

Then on to Stage 3: "Reintegration." Now our Babbitt "shows a tendency to internalize positive attitudes about majority groups as victims of reverse discrimination." He still "believes we are all the same" and prattles on: "I believe that quotas of any kind are wrong."

And so on through Stage 4, "Pseudo-independence"— "believes that discrimination is a problem of the uneducated" —until the final change of consciousness, the satori of Stage 5: "Autonomy"! Now he "accepts, respects, and appreciates both minority and majority individuals." And even better, he is given to making statements like this: "I am a recovering sexist."

Wait till the guys around the water cooler hear that! But Autonomy is an open-ended stage, for once there this new Babbitt, the one whose consciousness has at last been changed, also can say, "I accept the 'onion theory' that I will continue to peel away layers of my own racism for the rest of my life." The work, in other words, continues, forever. Which makes those long-range $500,000–a-year contracts absolutely imperative.

Enthusiasts for the New Age have known since the earliest days at Esalen that consciousness changing is a tricky task, beyond the poor power of mere lectures to accomplish. The sheep must be made to see and feel and *experience* their own part in the culture's larger evil; this is the "work" of the workshop. In diversity training, the purpose of lectures (or "lecturettes," as facilitators call them) is largely suggestive: they lay out the premises, establish an ideological context, so the sheep know what responses are expected of them. The real work involves experiential exercises—role playing, simulations, and other techniques of personal-growth therapy—that will, one hopes, crack open the dam of discussion.

This was the point of Bafa Bafa, the "cross-culture simulation," which I briefly thought might be the work of Allen Funt. Bafa Bafa simulates a clash of cultures. Workshoppers are separated into two groups, or cultures, and instructed in the customs of the group to which they've been assigned. These are elaborate and far-fetched, involving cards and poker chips and a specific language ("Bafa," "ro," "yo," etc.), and not particularly worth repeating here. Workshoppers then visit the other culture in pairs, via the imaginary bus, and return to their fellows to report on what they've seen. In time the groups are reunited, and then it's time for . . . *Let's talk!*

Like all simulations, Bafa Bafa is meant to be a "metaphor," and the facilitator's job is to ensure that nobody misses the point. As it turned out, my fellow workshoppers were already well versed in diversity dogma. The woman who felt fear and loneliness, and then felt compelled to share it with us, was responding on cue, and confirming the facilitator's earlier discourse about the tenacity with which the powerful hold on to power and the arrogance of white-male ethnocentrism.

But it is not always so easy for the poor facilitators! Sometimes, the room can be festooned with wall charts, the overhead projector casting pie charts onto the screen, the videos being shown—it's indisputable, very scientific, all laid out like a recipe—and *still* the Babbitts won't open up. They sit stone-faced, resentful. Not a feeling gets shared, not one racist sensation gets owned up to. The encounter-group discussions have the life energy of a can of tuna. That's when you bring in the heavy artillery.

You can make them dance. Yes, dance! Make the old white guys get down into their bodies and do the shimmy shake! Or you can paste little note cards to their foreheads, to make them *feel* the sense of being different. Or this one: You can break the workshoppers into five groups and pass out mug shots, one to each group, of an Asian woman, a Hispanic man, a Babbitt, and two other types—a black man or woman, say, or maybe a guy from a Calvin Klein ad if you're trying to work on heterosexism barriers. Then you present each group with the same scenario, detailing some work infraction committed by the fictional man or woman in the picture. Then ask the members of each group how they would deal with this malefactor.

It can be beautiful! If the group with the Babbitt's picture lets him off easy—easier than the others—well, then, come on, you don't need a flow chart to show what's behind that kind of kid-glove treatment. The old boy network! But sometimes it turns out that a group will treat the fictional white guy more harshly. (Yes: sometimes a few wiseacres can try to queer a workshop.) Anyway, no problem! It's clear: The group is holding the white-male to a higher standard. It's the stereotype: We expect white males to be competent, in control, brimming with integrity, and when one falls short of the stereotype—wham!—we lower the boom. Either way the workshoppers see, all at once, how they share in the power structure's intolerance of diversity.

Maybe that exercise seems a little tough, a bit too confrontational—well, try Diversity Bingo. You can get it mail order, from a company out in San Diego. For $99.95 you get an instruction booklet, fifty bingo cards, and a sixty-five-page facilitator's booklet with ready-made lecturettes and tips on debriefing the sheep. It's proved enormously popular. It's played like regular bingo. Every workshopper gets a bingo card. But instead of numbers, the little squares contain personal descriptions: "gay male," "person with high school education," "person over sixty," and so on. Card in hand, each workshopper approaches his fellows to ask: "Are you a gay male?" "Are you over sixty?" If the respondent says yes, he initials the card. The first person to fill up a consecutive string of boxes on the card wins—wins in a noncompetitive, nonhierarchical way, of course. Bingo!

Oh, how this loosens up the tight asses! Imagine going up to the company veteran, the old fart from Accounting with the two kids in college and the stay-at-home wife and the mortgage almost paid up, and watching his mouth twist into a grotesque little grin and the shine starting on his forehead, and then you get to ask him, point blank: "Are you gay!" Delicious! And he can't do a damn thing about it—because this is all for the bottom line.

And then the facilitator starts the encounter-group discussion. Let's talk! The mail-order package gives him a list of questions. Everyone sits in a circle. The facilitator goes around the group, asking the workshoppers one by one: "How do you feel about everyone who was different from you?" "How do you think others perceived you?" "How did you feel asking people their age—their education level—their sexual orientation?" Watch the old fart from Accounting squirm now! He's thinking: What the hell! This can't be happening. He's looking around for Allen Funt. His forehead's shining like molten wax, and that twisted quivering little grin slides across his face like an earthworm. How did he *feel*? And he doesn't know! Never thought about it. Well, welcome to the New Age, you clueless old fart! You relic! Oh, you Babbitt!

A diversity trainer, when he's really rolling, can offer up an almost infinite list of the ways we are all different. Aside from the obvious—race, sex, ethnicity—the diversity trainer will tell you about hair and eye color, left- or righthandedness, geographic background, age, weight, marital status . . . on and on.

But in truth there is one great divide separating us—placing on one side of the chasm people who love to sit in a circle and play experiential games and do personal-growth exercises and then talk about their feelings at great length, and people who don't. This divide cuts across lines of class and sex and age and ethnicity. And there's no question—to switch metaphors—who's got the upper hand. The naturally reticent, the people who cling to antique notions of privacy and personal dignity, who feel uneasy about turning the rough-and-tumble gridiron of American commerce into Mr. Rogers's Neighborhood, will either give in or be left behind.

What a curious thing this white-male power structure is! My facilitator may have mused that a "force situation" would someday become necessary. But my bet is that he needn't worry. The revolution proceeds without a shot being fired, with scarcely a peep of protest. In the history of power structures, the white-male power structure of late-twentieth-century America must be the strangest of all: the first to pay people to dismantle itself.

A Coffee Thing

November 1994

THIS IS A PIECE ABOUT COFFEE—DRINKING it, buying it, using it for ulterior purposes. It's also about a kind of snootiness that quickly flips into reverse snobbery, which sooner or later flips again into reverse-reverse snobbery, leaving the snob exhausted and confused. I myself am exhausted and confused—as you can tell.

In the early eighties I lived in a university town in the midwest. Like all such communities it was an uneasy mixture of town and gown. On the main street the pickups cruised slowly past the Volvos; in the neighborhoods the "U.S. Out of El Salvador" lawn signs coexisted with the "U.S. Out of the U.N." stickers in the front window next door. You could get your hair cut for $3.50 (no tip) at Sam's Barber Shop, or get it styled for $10 at Shear Delites Unisex Cuttery.

And you could drink coffee at Carl's Coffee Cup, or you could drink coffee at the Calico Munchkin. At Carl's coffee was a quarter. At the Munchkin the "house blend" sold for sixty-five cents, although most customers would choose a purer brew from a country squirming in the grip of Western imperialism. At Carl's your coffee was brought by a postmenopausal waitress with a pencil stuck in her bouffant. At the Munchkin you were served by a bouncing sophomore in a tube top, who more often than not forgot to charge you.

I had just moved from San Francisco. There everyone was a coffee snob. While most Americans might use a Mr. Coffee, for example, none of my acquaintances owned one; most had espresso machines, or some black lacquer turbine spouting fearsome tubes and pressure valves designed by (who else?) the Germans. Others used the Melitta method, in which the specially ground coffee was arranged at a precisely measured angle relative to the incoming water so as to maximize the exposure of the grounds while slowing the filtering process . . . or something. In any case, I'd caught the bug—bad. By the time I arrived at the university, my snobbery was intense and unremitting; my coffee had to be dark and rich, deeply aromatic, strong as a plow horse. Far more important, it had to mark me as a man above the herd.

By inclination, then, I was, so to say, a Munchkin man. Each morning for the first several months I would spread my *New York Times* before me and imbibe cup after cup of some Calico Munchkin specialty. On every side would sit professors in work shirts, turtlenecks, or woolen sweaters, their awestruck students miming their every move as they scraped chunks of banana-bran muffin from their beards. Back then, in the early eighties, they would speak confidently of Nicaragua's rising literacy rates, Israeli barbarism, ketchup as a vegetable! At last one morning I overheard a circle of grad students chortling over some witticism—no one told "jokes" in the Calico Munchkin—and the thought hit me with full force: *"These people laugh through their noses."* And I thought: *"I can't stand these people."* I thought: *"I hate these people."*

At once my snobbery did a one-and-a-half gainer and landed belly-side up. Suddenly the thought of being a Munchkin man chilled me. In a matter of days I had decamped, permanently, to Carl's. It is difficult to describe the coffee at Carl's: as you sipped it words like "resin" and "road kill" suggested themselves. I didn't mind, for my coffee drinking was still serving its primary purpose, which was to set me apart from people I held in derision. I flattered myself that I remained above the herd; it was just a different, smaller, and more contemptible herd—the "herd of independent minds," in Harold Rosenberg's phrase. And besides, I really did prefer the company, if not the coffee, at Carl's. To most of the patrons the idea of ketchup as a vegetable seemed pretty damn commonsensical.

Coffee snobbery transcends coffee; its pull is stronger than the sternest double cappuccino. I have been a reverse coffee snob for almost a decade now, pretending to savor the prole aroma of Folgers and Maxwell House. I even own a Mr. Coffee, with which I horrify my San Francisco friends when they come to visit. But now what? Look around: walk through any city neighborhood or suburb; travel beyond the yuppie enclaves, into deepest Illinois or Idaho. Coffee snobbery is America's fastest growing business. The Starbucks chain of coffee houses has grown like cancer from its native Seattle; its imitators are everywhere. People—not professors, not grad students, not yuppies, but *people*—now buy Sumatran Boengie at $5.50 a half pound, and order it ground to their specifications, and carry it home in little sacks, and gather round the Braun espresso machine in the kitchen to comment on the bean's earthy yet delicate balance of insouciant acidities.

All of America, in short, is turning into a giant Calico Munchkin. In the face of this new development, I am at a loss as to how to position myself. When the proles sip Ethiopian Harrar, profs and their legions will defect to Maxwell House. And I once again will be caught in the middle. The whipsaw effects of snobbery take their toll, and the only place for me may be the coffee snob's last refuge: to admit, once and for all, that I never much liked coffee in the first place.

Alice in Cyberland

June 1993

IMAGINE THE PARTY FROM HELL.

Imagine that your wife or husband has insisted on dragging you there. The room is overlit, the air heavy and damp with Lysol. Everyone is drinking Hawaiian Punch. You sidle up to one clump of guests, only to back away when you discover they're having a heated debate about the length of Lt. Uhura's miniskirt on *Star Trek*. The spittle flies. Another clump across the room debates the rutting habits of their pets. You edge away again, and bump into a fellow perched on the ottoman, raving to himself about J. Edgar Hoover's crossdressing.

You go to the CD player. Surely you can at least listen to some good music. Your eye scans the collection of CDs. *The Unreleased Trini Lopez. The Forgotten Years: Buddy Greco Live at the Copacabana. The Best of the Lennon Sisters, Vol. III.*

You're hungry. In the kitchen, the hostess is laying out the evening's hors d'oeuvres: Ding-Dongs with clam dip. Can you slip away to the study, to read a good book? You run your hands across the bookshelves—row after row of bound volumes of the *New York Times* op-ed page, circa 1979.

After seven or eight hours, the party ends. And then imagine that on the drive home, your wife or husband tells you that the two of you will be attending the same party every Saturday night for the rest of your lives.

If you can imagine this—if you can sense the crushing boredom, the frustration, the mind-numbing ennui—you have imagined your country's technological future. You have imagined life on the Information Superhighway.

The future wasn't supposed to be like this. For a decade the newsmagazines and talk shows, the hipper pundits and the most forward-looking pols have been unanimous in their enthusiasm for the Information Age. The future bestowed by the microchip and fiber optics was to be a kind of hopped-up democracy. Hierarchies would crumble as everyone gained the power to be in touch with everybody else all the time. Disembodied in the realm of cyberspace, freed of material constraints, human potential would be infinite. Soon everyone would use "access" as a verb and attach the prefix "cyber" to every conceivable noun.

Nobody can gainsay the advantages of the microchip, in banking, business, movie making, and a thousand other activities that have been streamlined and accelerated to the general good. But the benefits, too obvious and numerous to list, haven't quieted the carping of the mossbacks. I should admit that from time to time I've been skeptical too. This is partly owing to my fuddy-duddy instincts but also to experience. And I don't think my experience has been unusual.

My local library, to take one example, not long ago replaced its card catalogue with a database. Computer terminals now sit where once there were heavy wooden cabinets stuffed with index cards. At any given moment half the terminals are malfunctioning, and queues form at the others. In thirty years of using libraries, I've never before had to wait in line at a card catalogue.

A friend recently found work in a "paperless" office. It is now almost impossible to make a lunch date with him, since his datebook is computerized and it takes longer for him to check his schedule than to have lunch. And I've given up asking him for the phone numbers of mutual friends. He doesn't have a Rolodex anymore. He has an "information management system." It's somewhere in his computer. He's not sure where.

Well, well—I concede that these are merely provincial complaints. Those fearless cobblers who chose to leap into the Industrial Age probably had trouble with their shoemaking machines, too. By now every major government institution—from the Library of Congress to Congress itself—has caved to the compulsion to digitize itself, and it seems churlish, not to mention ruinously unhip, for anyone to resist any longer. Even me. The benefits sound irresistible: access to shopping, games, instant news, thousands of databases; the ability to make airline reservations and search for a restaurant without leaving your keyboard; membership in online forums to share ideas and gossip with thousands of like-minded folk; and electronic mail to communicate instantly with friends and strangers around the world.

And so last month I leapt into the future with both feet and, I like to think, an open mind. Now I am online. I fly through cyberspace. I speed down the Infobahn. I am firmly in the future. I want out.

The quickest and easiest way to suit up for an adventure in cyberspace is to join a commercial online service. For starters I joined two: CompuServe and its chief rival, America Online. I was impatient. After looking in the phone book (antediluvian) for the phone number and placing an order, I waited two weeks for the necessary software from Compu-Serve; AOL didn't arrive for another two days. CompuServe, then, was my introduction to cyberspace. I took the software upstairs to my computer and booted up. I was eager, almost breathless. My cynicism had vanished. E-mail! Databases! Interactivity! The future! Nothing!

My cursor winked-winked-winked in its taunting manner, and nothing happened. I hit <return>. Nothing. I hit <tab>. Nothing.

Then I remembered I hadn't hooked up my modem. For cybermorons, the Information Superhighway is a maze of such complications. Luckily, the CompuServe software is reasonably easy to load, and before too long I heard the annoying, scratchy static of the modem, and I was online.

I started to browse—this is also easy, since it requires only that you put the cursor on the word "browse" and hit <return>.

I went straight to News/Entertainment. For a journalist, one of the great advantages of being online is the ability to access news as it crosses the wire. I clicked on the AP headlines, updated hourly. President Clinton's health care reform was facing obstacles on Capitol Hill. I clicked on Entertainment News and read that Drew Barrymore was getting married. I clicked on Weather, and after scrolling through forty-seven of the fifty states, which took a little over a minute, I came to Virginia, where I live. CompuServe said it was hot. I stuck my head out the window. Exactly right!

I went to Research, and found my way to a menu that offers both the *American Heritage Dictionary* and *Grolier's* encyclopedia. I looked up the word "cyberspace" in the dictionary; after about sixty seconds of alarming grunts from my aged 286 computer, the screen showed that the word wasn't listed—slightly embarrassing, since at that moment I had an *American Heritage Dictionary* at my elbow, and I can generally work my way through the c's in fifteen seconds or less.

In the *Grolier's* I read the article about the Crimean War, because I know nothing about the Crimean War. It was informative—as informative, I eventually realized, as the article in my *Columbia Encyclopedia*, which is next to my dictionary and is already paid for.

I went back to Entertainment and accessed the Entertainment Encyclopedia. I was sorry to see that here there were only a handful of entries. I read a three-year-old interview with Gene Hackman, who mused at length about his "craft." Then I clicked on a complete listing of every nightly TV schedule from 1948 onward. I was surprised to discover in the listings for 1964 that *The Dick Van Dyke Show* was on *Wednesday* nights! I could have sworn it was Tuesday. Amazing! The remaining entry was a complete itinerary for every Beatles tour from 1962 through 1966. I passed. My eyes were starting to hurt.

I got up from the computer to stretch my legs. I had been in cyberspace for almost two hours. I felt the stirring of a headache behind my left eye. I was groggy, slightly dazed— as if I had just watched a dozen episodes of *Gilligan's Island* back to back. (When this analogy occurred to me, I suddenly remembered that, if I wanted to, I could find out on what night *Gilligan's Island* had originally aired. But I didn't want to.) After pacing awhile, I returned to the computer. Apparently I had let my machine sit idle too long. CompuServe had automatically signed me off.

I returned to CompuServe routinely night after night. I kept up with the news. President Clinton's health care reform faced obstacles on Capitol Hill. Drew Barrymore was on her honeymoon. The weather stayed hot. And I was getting cyber-discouraged. On both AOL and CompuServe I tried to buy an airline ticket to Chicago for my brother's wedding in August. Both employ a service called EAASY SABRE, which is affiliated with American Airlines. You have to apply for membership, but I could never get past the application form. I'd fill out my name and address and then would try to <tab> to "OK." The cursor inevitably returned me to "Cancel," and I'd have to start all over again. In my discouragement I fantasized that the computer was doing a lightning-fast credit check and rejecting me immediately. These computers are pretty smart. I ended up calling my travel agent, who got me a great fare. Within ten minutes.

I'm not big on games, but friends had told me of the inter-active entertainments available in cyberspace, and I tried a few. Most of the games seem to be the kind favored by fellows who spent long winter afternoons after school playing Dungeons and Dragons. They're heavy on gothic story telling, with lots of damsels, hidden treasures, and spooky houses.

Castlequest, for example, which is available on Compu-Serve's basic package, is a narrative game that opens with a very long description of the Carpathian Mountains, through which the player is supposedly traveling. His car breaks down. It is dark, of course, and stormy, and the narrative drops the player into a spooky castle. "The object of the game is to find the master of the castle and deal with him as needed, while looting the castle of its treasures."

There are no graphics on Castlequest, only text. The player is told he is awakening in a bed in a room in the castle. Then the interactive part begins. A question mark flashes on the screen, to which you are supposed to respond.

I typed: "Let's go."

"I don't think I understand," the computer replied.

I typed: "Move."

"I don't think I understand," the computer replied.

I typed: "Get up."

"I don't think I understand."

I typed: "Quit."

"Score: 0! You are a greenhorn at this game!"

I typed: "Go to hell." But the game was over and I had been returned to the main menu.

After a while you begin to suspect that cyberspace is con-structed for a particular type of person: specifically, as I say, those people who used to spend long hours playing Dungeons and Dragons—until, of course, their parents bought them computers.

The suspicion lingers, despite the mainstream trappings of the commercial online services. Even beyond the restaurant reviews, movie reviews, airline reservations, and e-mail, the trappings are vast and numerous. There are those thousands of databases, of course, narrowcasted for highly specific professional or avocational interests. They are difficult to access and can be very expensive. Both AOL and CompuServe play to the news junkies by offering a newsmagazine online—*U.S. News & World Report* for CompuServe, *Time* for AOL. I read the first few issues of each after I came online. President Clinton's health care plan was facing obstacles on Capitol Hill, and Drew Barrymore announced she was getting a divorce. Reading the magazines was cumbersome, though. In cyberform a newsmagazine is very hard to scan—and does anyone do more than scan newsmagazines in the Information Age?

AOL's basic package offers highbrow magazines, too. For anyone with a yen to read an eight-thousand-word article about, say, ethnographic trends in Kuala Lumpur, the *Atlantic Monthly* is online. If you want up-to-date reflections on homosexual marriage, gays in the military, the case for bourgeois homosexuality, or the history of gay rights radicalism, you can get the *New Republic* on AOL. CompuServe offers access to Ziffnet, a database containing more than a thousand magazines. Ziffnet charges $1.50 to call up a single article on your screen, another $1.50 to print it out. You don't need a calculator function on your computer to figure out that you could probably buy the whole magazine for less.

But these services are mere gloss. The essence of the Information Superhighway is better revealed by the interactive communications among those who travel it. Cyberspace is choked with conferences and "chat rooms" and "town halls" and "forums"—microcosmic venues where people interact onscreen in "real time." Sign on to one of these and your screen shows the dialogues as they take place. And everyone is encouraged to join in by tapping out a message at the bottom of his screen.

There are forums for every conceivable taste. Not long ago, to some fanfare, the Republican party opened up a "Republican" forum on CompuServe. I used to be a Republican, so I signed on. A little read-out tells you the name of whoever else is signed on and where you can find them in the forum. Every time I visited, five or six soulmates were listed as being "in the lobby." None of them ever entered the "conference rooms," where they could type messages to one another. It conjured up a discouraging mental image: a handful of Republicans waiting outside a room, hands in pockets, eyes down, hoping that someone else would actually say something. A lot like the Republican party, as a matter of fact.

There are forums for journalists and Mustang owners, quilters and Russophiles, occultists and vegans. "Message boards" allow the adepts to post questions and comments for other members to read and answer as they wish. If, for example, you're looking for a new fuel gauge for your 1967 Mustang, you can post a query in hopes that some other Mustang lover will answer your need. If you don't own a Mustang, however, reading the forum will put you in a coma within minutes.

These specialized forums, say cybernauts, are creating "virtual communities," groups of self-selected, like-minded people who commune in the cyberworld unconstrained by time and space. For those who haven't yet advanced into a virtual community, AOL and CompuServe offer general-interest forums. Assign yourself an onscreen name—these generally veer toward the cute—and just sign on. But be warned: In cyberspace, "real time" is more accurately "lag time," which makes it difficult for anyone to interact sequen-

tially. In "Teen Chat" (AOL), for example, you might read
this exchange:

> Gem692: Bikini Kill rules.
> Peabrain: Is Quicksand online tonight?
> GunRose: Miss H. Locklear is soooooooo hot. . .
> Upchuck94: I'm a little high tonite, dudes.
> Gem692: Is the system slow or is it just me?
> RL658: Bikini Kill sucks!!!!!
> GunRose: hothothothothothot
> Quicksand: I'm here, Pea. How ya doin'?
> Peabrain: Is Quicksand here?
> Upchuck94: Wo, dude.
> GunRose: Any women on here tonite?

I wish I could report that this exchange was atypical—kids
today!—but its tone isn't much lower than what you'll find
in the other forums and chat rooms. Messages are restricted
to two lines apiece; as a consequence, the ideas expressed tend
to be . . . *uncomplicated*. And redundant. And eventually
numbing. Before long you'll be yearning for *Gilligan's Island*.

On most forums, incidentally, the answer to GunRose's last
question—any women here tonite?—is very often no. This
makes cyberflirting, much less cybersex, extremely problematic. (Cybersex, which has been subject to much examination in the press, is problematic for other reasons, too: How
fast can you type with one hand?) Owing to the nature of the
technology, cybertalk is blunt and quick and unreflective—
male characteristics, every one—and flirting forums quickly
take on the tone of a late-night gripe session in a men's dorm:
"*Where the hell are all the babes?*" The answer, of course, is
that most of "the babes" are out with men who don't spend
their evenings in front of a computer terminal.

* * *

Contrary to its deep-thinking apologists, the Information
Superhighway is not destroying all hierarchies; it is simply
creating a new one. You see hints of it in the fevered meta-
physics extolled by devoted cybersurfers. Online and in
magazines, they differentiate between their "meat bodies"—
by which they mean corporeal bodies—and their "cyber-
doppelgangers," their true selves as projected into cyberspace.
They talk dismissively of "RL" (real life) and spin visions of
parallel worlds. This talk will be familiar to anyone who
attended an American high school. The future has fallen into
the hands of the kids who ran the Audio-Visual Club—the guys
with the shiny foreheads and the acne and the coke-bottle
glasses and the highwater pants, who played video games for
weeks at a time and attended Star Trek conventions. They
were pariahs then; they are the gatekeepers today. Cyberspace is where they mean to get even.

This unnerving truth is made plain from a few hours on
the Internet, the Beltway of the Information Superhighway.
Originally a link among university databases and the federal
government, the Net has grown helter-skelter to include, by
some estimates, more than ten million users worldwide, clus-
tered around at least two thousand virtual communities, or
"newsgroups," as they're called on the Net. It is unimaginably
vast, chaotic, and confusing.

The best way to jump in is through one of the smaller
online services. Although access to lots of stuff on the Internet
itself is free, the cost of getting there is steep: Delphi, the service I used, charges $4 an hour, after a $25 registration fee;
during business hours, access to the phone lines is an additional $9 an hour. Free information can be expensive.

But it can be fun, too—for a while. On the Net you can surf
newsgroups according to taste. In any given group, thousands
of messages will be posted from users in any country with
electricity. Naturally, as a reporter for a general interest

magazine, I first headed for the newsgroup with the greatest general interest: "alt.sex." The offerings were not for the timid. Among the topics to which the cyberphiles had posted messages: "Sex in graveyards," "Best songs to have sex to," "How to prolong orgasms," "CDs of real people having real sex." Several headings broached the subject of why there weren't more women on the Net. The topic heading with the most messages was, not surprisingly, "I can't get laid."

The databases offer everything from the complete works of Shakespeare to explications of Einstein's General Theory. These databases are the black holes of the Highway—once you fall in, you may be there for hours. One night around 2 A.M. I found myself in a database that could download the original lyrics to "Louie, Louie." I don't have the slightest idea how I got there, and I have no intention of going back.

In fact, I'm quitting cyberspace altogether. It is no place for a fuddy-duddy. You begin to wonder what all this is *for*. On the Net and elsewhere, I've read the solemn pronouncements about "free access to killer info" and a New Age of microcosmic populism. But I still can't figure out why, for example, we should prefer to read the local paper on our computers when we can get an old-fashioned and less-expensive newsprint version delivered to our doorstep.

I remember the moment when my disenchantment with the Information Age became irreversible. I had flipped on AOL one night and joined a celebrity forum. The special guests were Shari Lewis and Lamb Chop. The questions from out in cyberspace came fast and furious, for both guests, and the reality of the thing hit me all at once: from coast to coast, people with the intelligence to operate computers were actually sitting at home and conversing with a *hand puppet*. This, I realized, is the future the A-V guys have created for us. This is the revenge of the nerds.

I'm Terrific,
You're Terrific

May 1995

NOBODY I KNOW OF HAS YET SUGGESTED THAT
Timothy McVeigh, the indicted Oklahoma City bomber, suf-
fers from low self-esteem, but surely it's only a matter of
time. Watch for his lawyer or some rent-an-expert shrink
trying to snow the trial jury. Or maybe it will be Oprah—
Oprah, that is, in the generic sense, as in one of the dozens
of daytime talk-show Barnums whose job it is to display
America's freaks in order to massage the emotions of TV-
addled stay-at-homes. Perhaps McVeigh himself will take
the stage, and tearfully recount the beatings from a psycho
dad, the icy stares of his boozebag mom, and from the audience Oprahphilsallyjessygeraldo will immediately spot yet
another instance of the age's malady, the dysfunction of the
decade: *Tim—may I call you Tim?—your problem is you
don't like yourself.*

You think I exaggerate? Self-esteem is to our day what
"iron-poor blood" or "an attack of the humours" was to earlier times. It is the all-purpose cause and effect, a will-o'-the-
wisp rationale that explains every event, exculpates every
transgressor. It is, to speak mildly, overused. When I trolled
through a database of newspapers and magazines, limiting
myself to a two-week period in April, the term popped up

more than 550 times, including four mentions in a single edition of the *Atlanta Journal-Constitution*, two each for the current *Fortune* and *Mothering* magazines, three for *Billboard*, and a whopping seven for *Essence*. Different writers writing different articles on wildly different subjects: all had reached instinctively for the buzziest of buzzwords.

Did you know, for example, that according to one expert the recent war between Ecuador and Peru was a blow to the Peruvian military's "self-esteem"? (War *is* hell.) A school counselor in a Chicago suburb concluded that a student had murdered his best friend's parents because of his "low self-esteem." A urologist announced that the epidemic of low self-esteem among men could be eradicated by a surgical procedure known as "penis augmentation." After the Los Angeles Municipal Transit Authority awarded an $80 million contract to a bogus construction firm, a blue ribbon investigation traced the scandal to "a low level of self-esteem" among the staff. And when asked about the motives of the notorious Unabomber, a San Francisco psychiatrist put it this way: "People like this tend to suffer from a tremendous lack of self-esteem." Ka-boom.

This supposed plague of low self-esteem is not limited to mail bombers, murderers, inept bureaucrats, and guys with teeny-weeny weenies. "Most of us are children of dysfunctional families," writes the Father of the Self-Esteem Movement, Nathaniel Branden, which means therefore that most of us suffer from low self-esteem, which in turn guarantees land-office business for Dr. Branden. From every side Americans are encouraged to goose their self-esteem. Leafing through a local "parenting" magazine, for example, you will read: "We have to be content with ourselves before we have the ability to truly give to our children." This is one of the neatest philosophical tropes of the self-esteem movement: self-absorption as altruism. It reached its fullest, and most popular, expression in Whitney Houston's mawkish anthem, "The Greatest Love of All." Love of whom? You shouldn't have to ask.

> *Everybody's searching for a hero.*
> *People need someone to look up to.*
> *I never found anyone who fulfilled my needs,*
> *So I learned to depend on me. . . .*
> *The greatest love of all is easy to achieve.*
> *Learning to love yourself—*
> *It is the greatest love of all.*

I needn't add that the song went double platinum and has since become a staple of Superbowl half-time shows, Olympic extravaganzas, and kids' concerts in school assembly halls from one end of the country to the other. No wonder we hate us.

And let's assume that we do. Let's assume that everybody's self-esteem is in the toilet, wreaking every manner of social havoc. This raises the inconvenient question, "What are we talking about?" What, in short, is this thing called self-esteem?

Unfortunately, the last place you can find an answer to the question is in the vast literature of self-esteem—the endless rows of self-help manuals, feel-good advice books, and pseudoscientific treatises that choke the psychology sections of every chain bookstore in the country. Perhaps it's more accurate to say that while you can't find *an* answer, you can find dozens of answers, hundreds even.

I will bore you with only a few, from which you can easily catch the drift. Stanley Coopersmith's *The Antecedents of Self-Esteem:* "Self-esteem is a personal judgment of worthiness that is expressed in the attitudes the individual holds toward himself." From *Self-Esteem: Paradoxes and Innovations in*

Clinical Theory and Practice: "We define self-esteem as a subjective and endearing sense of realistic self-approval." From a California state government report: "Self-esteem is defined as: Appreciating my own worth and importance. . . ." From educationist Frederick Krieg: "Self-esteem is the filter we use to see how we feel about ourselves." And Nathaniel Branden himself, progenitor of the movement, says this: "I want you to know precisely what I mean when I say 'self-esteem.' Self-esteem is the experience that we are appropriate to life and to the requirements of life."

Did he say "precisely"? Though they share certain elements—an emphasis on the subjective nature of self-esteem, for instance—these definitions are united most of all by their almost unfathomable vagueness. And the literature, both pop and scholarly, exploits the vagueness to the limit. Do you burst into tears at odd moments? You probably suffer from low self-esteem. Are you one of those hairy-chested fellows who never cries? Sounds like a self-esteem problem. Are you too aggressive? Low self-esteem. Too shy? Your self-esteem needs a serious tune-up. And so on, and so on.

At once infinitely elastic and infinitely important-sounding, explaining everything from bad manners to homicide, self-esteem is perfectly suited for the theoreticians of the American educational system. Here is where the vogue has taken deepest root. Educational theory has already inflated the language with such gassy participles as "mentoring," "modeling," and "therapizing." "Esteeming" is next. In education schools, everybody sounds like Newt Gingrich reading from a book by Alvin and Heidi Toffler.

In her hair-raising examination of such places, *Ed School Follies*, the journalist Rita Kramer discovered that the "reigning educational philosophy" is now "self-esteem," although the word "philosophy" is probably inappropriate. Over the years the function of ed schools, from which most of America's teachers issue forth, has been to alter "the teacher's role from source of knowledge to classroom manager of a learning cooperative designed to provide experiences that will enhance students' self esteem." The educationist Fred Krieg, using the sing-songy phrases that delight today's grad students of education, says the ideal teacher is a "guide by the side, not a sage on the stage." The results will be familiar to most parents with students in public school: the abandonment of "tracking,"the devaluation or outright elimination of grades, the trend away from the transmission of objective facts toward the inculcation of subjective feelings. The technique of "inventive spelling," for example, has become widely popular, allowing students in the first few years of grade school to spell words "in any way that feels right to them." One student-teacher explained to Kramer why she refused to teach her second-grade students unfamiliar vocabulary words: "The main thing is for them to feel good about themselves as readers."

Such inventiveness has saturated the schools for several years, and its most famous consequence was explored by a researcher at the University of Michigan, Harold Stevenson. "When asked to rate such characteristics as ability in mathematics, brightness, and scholastic performance, American children gave themselves the highest ratings, while Japanese students gave themselves the lowest." Objective international rankings, of course, are precisely the reverse, with the Japanese on top and the Yanks in the cellar. In one international achievement test, American thirteen-year-olds performed the worst of all those tested in mathematics; at the same time, their own estimation of their math skills was higher than any other thirteen-year-olds tested.

Stevenson's widely publicized findings, and others like them, created a stir—so much so that for a brief moment, in the early nineties, it looked as if a self-esteem backlash might occur. The movement wasn't helped by California's famous "Task Force to Promote Self-Esteem and Personal and Social Responsibility." Empaneled by the state legislature in 1986, the task force tacked the "responsibility" onto its title in hopes of calming the objections of reactionaries—but to no avail. Even "Doonesbury" lampooned the effort as the ultimate expression of California flightiness. Matters were made even worse when the task force released its report and the underlying scientific data it had accumulated.

The task force's premise was the one still held dear today, from Oprah to the ed schools, that almost every social pathology—teen pregnancy, drug and child abuse, poor school performance, the works—could be traced to a lack of self-esteem in individuals. After a close reading of the data, however, the report's editors reached a grim conclusion: "One of the disappointing aspects of every chapter in this volume . . . is how low the associations between self-esteem and its consequences are in the research to date." And grimmer: "If the association between self-esteem and behavior is so often reported to be weak, even less can be said for the causal relationship between the two."

As the psychological researcher Robyn Dawes points out in *House of Cards: Psychology and Psychotherapy Built on Myth*, this last statement was even more devastating than the report's editors acknowledged. Were there a causal relationship between self-esteem and certain kinds of behavior, some correlation should have shown up in the statistical data. And because no such correlation could be shown, it's safe to conclude that self-esteem, high or low, does not in itself cause any particular behavior, good or bad.

As we've seen, even self-esteem's biggest boosters have trouble defining the term; objective researchers find the task close to impossible. It is difficult, in fact, to give the phrase any objective content at all. Still, in light of the thousands of studies done on self-esteem, some conclusions are pretty firm, particularly in the supposed relationship between self-esteem and academic achievement. The ed school credo asserts that

raising self-esteem will bring higher levels of academic performance. No such relationship is supported by the research,
which was well summarized by Thomas Moeller of Mary
Washington College.

First, writes Moeller, "in the early elementary years, performance causes academic self-concept [a high-brow term for
self-esteem] rather than the other way around." As for the high
school years, "what is clear from a variety of studies is that
global self-concept does not cause academic achievement."
And finally: "Academic performance seems to be more related
to children's ability to set academic standards and to persist in
trying to meet them than it is to their self-esteem, however that
concept may be defined."

This tends to affirm the hoary conventional wisdom of old-
fashioned squares—which is that "self-esteem" is a by-product
rather than a cause of achievement. A student's opinion of himself improves as his performance improves. In other words, if
you want a student to feel good about himself, teach him to
do something well. Self-esteem will take care of itself.

In fact, some studies of middle school children indicate that
there may be a *negative* relationship between "global self-
concept," or self-esteem, and academic performance. The
psychologist William Damon makes the case that many of
the more vacuous self-esteem efforts—for example, hand-
ing out buttons that say "I'm Terrific" to school kids—may
indeed lower their self-esteem. "Some children develop an
exaggerated, though empty and ultimately fragile, sense of
their own powers," he writes in his book *Greater Expecta-
tions.* "Some dissociate their feelings of self-worth from any
conduct that they are personally responsible for. . . . Other
children develop a skepticism about such statements and
become increasingly inured to positive feedback of any kind.
In time this can generalize into a distrust of adult communications and a gnawing sense of self-doubt." Self-*doubt?* Oops.

* * *

Here, then, is where matters stand: Large numbers of responsible adults are making assertions that are either meaningless or untrue, soaking up large amounts of public and private resources to advance their erroneous or meaningless
assertions, and then trying to impose the half-baked notions
on the nation's children, not to mention daytime talk-show
audiences. Aristotle, in brief, has been dumped for Oprah.
How did this happen?

The possible answers range from the innocent to the slightly
sinister. America today has engulfed itself in a Cult of the Kid—
a romantic celebration of the uncluttered "genius" of childhood. This is not to be confused with our national "obsession
with youth," another staple of Phil Donahue deepthink and
newsmagazine cover stories. Our obsession with youth—as
demonstrated, for example, in clothing advertisements and the
fad of liposuction—is rooted in a desire for supple bodies, lots
of leisure time, and a release from the pressures of mortality.
It is at least semirational. Kidcult is not. Kidcult is based on
the premise that children, notwithstanding their bad grammar
and terrible personal hygiene, are somehow in touch with a
timeless wisdom that we adults have forgotten. The premise
is shared by the self-esteem movement, which advises us to
coddle the kids and never be so bold as to correct their mistakes. "Let the children lead the way," sings Whitney Houston in her anthem. "If you want to understand Earth Day," a
Washington Post Style writer oozed not long ago, "talk to a
kid." And of course our first lady has published a book called
It Takes a Village and Other Lessons Children Teach Us.

The problem is, children don't have anything to teach us.
True, they are not silly in the way adults are often silly; only
an adult, for example, could have concocted the first lady's
National Health Care Plan. But in general kids are stupid. They
go for years without knowing how to tie their shoes. Their
stupidity is why we don't let them drive or write checks. Until
1993, in fact, they couldn't even be hired for high-ranking

jobs at the White House. The original idea of education was that school could cure their stupidity. But this was before the stupidity was mistaken for a primal wisdom that is best left undisturbed.

Reinforced by Kidcult, the self-esteem movement has several practical benefits for teachers, administrators, counselors, social workers, and the other professionals we pay to handle our children for us. If the chief task of schools is learning, the transmission and absorption of facts, then success or failure can be easily measured. And in recent years the schools' failure in this regard has been measured all too clearly. But if the purpose of education is therapy, the cultivation of subjective feelings, then objective measurements are worthless—an exercise in irrelevant rationality. Everybody is off the hook. Schools emulate Lake Wobegon, where all the children are above average.

Dig further into the self-esteem literature, however, descend past the fuzzy-wuzzy clichés and the Kidcult propaganda, and you come upon (surprise!) a political agenda. The self-esteem booster and educationist James A. Beane notes that the political rationale for self-esteem is seldom employed publicly, the better to avoid unnecessary controversy. Nevertheless, wrote Beane in an influential article in *Educational Leadership* magazine, "only the most ignorant or arrogant could fail to see that we face increasing problems with inequitable distribution of wealth, power, justice, racism, sexism, poverty, and homelessness. . . . The resolution of these issues will depend less on rhetoric and more on action, but action is not likely unless people believe they can make a difference. . . . Enhancing self-esteem helps build the personal and collective efficacy that helps us out of the morass of the inequity that plagues us."

In this view, self-esteem becomes a way of generating legions of mini–Ralph Naders, as if the big one we already have weren't one too many. "Work with self-esteem," continued Beane, "offers the possibility that young people will challenge the status quo." Thus, in schools that properly value self-esteem, "a premium would be placed upon collaborative teacher-student planning, cooperative learning, thematic units that emphasize personal and social meanings, student self-evaluation, multicultural content, community service projects, and activities that involve making, creating and 'doing'"—everything, it seems, but reading, writing, and 'rithmetic (and geography, spelling, history. . .).

The fundamentally political purpose of the self-esteem movement is shown most vividly by Gloria Steinem, who stormed the bestseller lists a couple of years ago with *Revolution from Within: A Book of Self-Esteem*. Like much of the literature, it is a shapeless grab-bag of confession, exhortation, and theory. Her thesis remains the feminist axiom, "The personal is political," leavened now with the idea, borrowed from the self-esteem movement, that self-absorption is altruistic. The enlightened person thinks constantly about himself not because he is a selfish boor but because he wants to serve others. Assuming he has time.

Self-esteem, writes Steinem, is "a birthright that can only be preserved by transforming education and child-rearing; by abandoning patriarchy, racial caste systems, monotheism, and hierarchy as the main form of human organization; indeed by transforming Western civilization itself." It's hard to imagine a more comprehensively political agenda than this. And it's true that only someone who thinks he's pretty terrific should attempt it. (Kids, *please* don't try this at home.)

Since the source of low self-esteem lies in Western civilization itself, Steinem turns to the Mysterious East for the means to raise self-esteem—specifically to the practice of "meditation." An appendix to *Revolution* offers a do-it-yourself guide for the reader who wants to plumb the depths. Anyone familiar with Asian forms of meditation will find the

Steinemized version almost unrecognizable; you could even, if you were unkind, call it "Westernized." In Buddhist meditation, for example, the idea is to empty your head of received ideas, to "transcend thought." Whether this is possible is another question, but it has a certain kind of philosophical integrity. The meditation that Steinem encourages—a technique known as visualization, in which the meditator imagines himself as a child, then as a "future self," etc.—aims to empty the mind of all thoughts but one: Me. What do I want? What's good for me? In keeping with the ideology of self-esteem, it raises self-absorption to the level of metaphysical virtue.

And the purpose of this, in turn, is political. Through various case studies, Steinem shows how self-absorption, properly guided, can turn to . . . *anger.* "Now when things don't work," says one successful meditator, "I get mad instead of depressed." Terrific! And the anger is always directed outward—at those caste systems, hierarchies, and patriarchies that grind us all. Or some of us, anyway. Anger leads to action, to marches and organizing and pamphleting the local Safeway. Thus does meditation, whose traditional purpose is the wisdom of silence, become a means of resolving the unequal distribution of income. What hath the Buddha wrought?

If it all sounds slightly unreasonable, it's supposed to. Perhaps the most revealing comment made during the steady advance of the self-esteem movement came from John Vasconcellos, the California state assemblyman who got the bright idea for his state's task force on self-esteem. When its report showed no relationship between self-esteem and the countless troubles it was supposed to solve, Vasconcellos dismissed all criticism. Criticism, he said, came "from those who only live in their heads, in the intellectual."

Well, we'll be having no more of that. Certainly not on *Oprah*, and certainly not in the schools. You can even see the outlines of the new all-purpose excuse taking shape. "I'm sorry, Your Honor," the defendant could say. "I was just living so much in my head. It was like reason had me by the throat. I couldn't feel straight." In time Tim McVeigh's lawyers will get wise, and all of us will learn to see their client as a slave to logic, a victim of reason, denied the Greatest Love of All.

Dumbing Down

October 1993

IN JULY THE EDUCATIONISTS OF FAIRFAX
County, Virginia, banned class rankings in three of their high
schools. Other schools, it's assumed, will soon follow. Fairfax
students will thus escape an unpleasantness that generations
before them suffered—the damp palms and night sweats that
come from the oppressive expectation that you should do well
and have a standing to show for it. Unburdening the kids in
this way was surely meant as an act of kindness. It was also
an act that helps define the decade. It was a very nineties thing
to do.

Cultural commentators, academics, and other chin-pullers
have worried that this decade lacks distinctive shape and
flavor—a *zeit* with no *geist*. In assigning blame, some go
straight to the top: A president who changes policy positions
by the hour and a first lady with more hairdos than Madonna
can't be expected to impress their identities on a decade, since
no one knows what those identities are. Other eggheads say
the problem lies in the country itself, grown too fractious and
atomized to be summed up with a single theme.

Earlier decades, in hindsight at least, are easy to define. The
fifties were tailfins and prosperity and white bread and Ike; the
sixties were Woodstock and Vietnam and civil rights. The seventies were the Me Decade and the eighties the Decade of Greed.
Zip-plop-clunk! The clichés fall reassuringly into place.

In hindsight, too, the anomalies of decade-defining become apparent. The poet Allen Ginsberg once pointed out that decades do not conform numerically: The sixties, for example, really began around 1963–64, with the death of JFK and the arrival of the Beatles, and ended in, say, 1974, with the defenestration of Richard Nixon. In the same way, today's historians should probably date the beginning of the nineties to the end of Reaganism, practically accomplished by late 1987, when the stock market crashed and the public learned the unseemly details of the arms sales to Iran.

The beast that rose from the ashes of the eighties is with us still. It comprises both George Bush and Bill Clinton, the programmers at PBS and the editors of *USA Today*, the Fairfax County school board and the owners of major-league baseball. All infuse the era with a common spirit. All are engaged, often unconsciously, in a great project of cultural leveling, a planing away of differences in wealth, status, effort, brains, and, as in Fairfax County, class rank, however you define class.

Referring to those who shaped the common culture in his own day, H . L . Mencken defined a Puritan as a person who lies awake nights fretting that someone, somewhere, might be having a good time. The tone-setters of the nineties are kin to the Puritans, sharing the same astringency and recti-tude. Their sleep is disturbed by a new obsession: the worry that someone, somewhere, might be getting ahead.

The nineties are the Dumbed-Down Decade. There isn't much doubt anymore that America is getting dumber and has been doing so for some time. What's less obvious, and unique to the nineties, are the feverish efforts to make the dumbing down seem as unalarming—indeed, as salutary—as possible.

The most vivid evidence of galloping stupidity comes, not surprisingly, from that wheezing old Edsel designed to make us all smarter, the American educational system. It's been a decade since the much-quoted, seldom-read report *A Nation at Risk* spoke of a "rising tide of mediocrity" in education. The nation's Scholastic Aptitude Test (SAT) scores have been on a downward path for twenty-five years: a drop from 466 to 423 in average verbal scores, from 492 to 476 in math. Every few years the National Assessment of Educational Progress and other surveys release yet another sad litany: Half the nation's seventeen-year-olds can't express the fraction 9/100 as a percentage; a quarter of them don't know that Congress is a legislative branch; almost half can't place the Civil War in the correct half-century.

Reports of this steady lobotomizing, as measured by objective tests, are followed by a chorus of sighs and calls for reform. But the nation's educators have orchestrated a more ingenious response: a subtle, even elegant campaign to disparage objective testing as divisive and unfair. The campaign has been an extraordinary success. By law, for example, the results of the National Assessment of Educational Progress could not be broken down beyond state-by-state rankings, meaning that no parent or educator can use the results to any practical effect: by, say, comparing one high school with another.

Similarly, the SATs have been redesigned to include fewer questions and allow more time to answer them. Students will be permitted to use calculators in the quantitative sections. Anything to get the scores up—although some educators have objected to this innovation as discriminatory against students who don't own calculators. For the verbal test, a proposal was made to include a mandatory essay question. Officials in California put the testing service on notice: The state would drop the SAT if an essay question were included. Such a question, they said, would "put some students at a disadvantage."

The campaign against testing fits with broader efforts to question the very idea of intelligence. That one person might be smarter than another, and that the difference might be measurable, are facts that today seem too invidious and "judgmental" (the decade's all-purpose epithet) for America's tender sensibilities. So prickly has the question become that California—again a bellwether—has prohibited some schoolchildren from taking IQ tests, even if their parents request it. The Department of Labor's Employment Service has shelved the General Aptitude Test Battery, a quasi-intelligence test that states had long used to determine the job qualifications of potential employees.

A less draconian approach among academics has been to argue that intelligence as commonly understood (the rational problem-solving ability that scholars call general intelligence) either doesn't exist or is simply one kind of intelligence among many. Thus physical coordination, or "kinesthetic bodily ability," can take its place alongside problem-solving as an equal manifestation of intelligence. (Nobody here but us smart guys!) The belief in "multiple intelligences" dovetails with the pleasant truism that everyone is good at something and extends it to the much more debatable proposition that whatever skill you're good at is as valuable as any other skill. In the words of one scholar, the notion of multiple intelligences "democratizes" intelligence.

This democratizing, as dumbing down often has come to be called, yields some curious practices, most familiar in the public schools. Fairfax's abandonment of class ranking is one example. Several schools have given up selecting class valedictorians, or have made the selection a matter of popular vote. In other public schools, traditional grades are becoming passé. Programs for "gifted" students have been transformed—banned from some schools as elitist, or made so democratic that the only criterion for admission is that the child's parents nominate him. Note, too, that the egalitarian etiquette of the nineties will increasingly require the use of

ironic quotation marks around elitist terms like "gifted" or
"achievement." In the sixties we had to do the same thing
with the word "reality."

As unreal as our educational system often is, it fairly reflects
the larger culture. Beyond the schoolyard, evidence of dumbing
down is as near as the corner newspaper box dispensing *USA
Today*. Journalists delight in ridiculing "The Nation's Newspaper" for its trivial news coverage, its tone of unremitting
cheerfulness, and its substitution of gorgeous graphics for sub-
stantive prose. (One joke popular in newsrooms: "Did you hear
USA Today finally won a Pulitzer? Best Investigative Paragraph!") But as a glance through most American newspapers
will show, the intensity of their contempt for the paper has been
matched only by their doggedness in emulating it.

   A common criticism of *USA Today* is that it seems modeled
on television, but that may be unfair to *USA Today*. Called a
vast wasteland thirty years ago, fit only for boobs and rubes,
television of the nineties has ironically created its own kind of
snob: a generation that yearns for the sophistication of Dobie
Gillis. The decline is seen most vividly on public television,
which was designed as a refuge from the lowest-common-
denominator bilge of the commercial networks. At public
television's founding in 1967, the essayist E. B. White wrote of
its potential to "arouse our dreams, satisfy our hunger for
beauty . . . to be our Chautauqua, our Lyceum." Mr. White,
lucky for him, is dead, and he has thus been spared the seem-
ingly monthly rite of "pledge week." At first, public television's
standard fare was a professor in white smock lecturing about
photosynthesis; it was called "educational TV." Now, during
pledge week, our modern Chautauqua flatters its viewers with
lengthy tributes to the Beatles, Bob Dylan, Peter, Paul & Mary,
and the Grateful Dead, not one member of which would know
the Lyceum from a roller derby.

But the Grateful Dead possesses at least one virtue: they're not Nirvana. Nirvana was the rock 'n' roll band that popularized "grunge"—a trend that, as one observer told the *New York Times*, "runs against the whole flashy esthetic that existed in the eighties." "It's not anti-fashion," said another. "It's unfashion." Specifically, it's monochordal music, matted hair, and hundreds of thousands of middle-class young people affecting attitudes of lethargy and boredom. Preferred dress is courtesy of St. Vincent de Paul: threadbare flannel shirts, large boots, and tattered jeans slung low, in the manner of home repairmen through the ages.

Though the term itself has been superseded, grunge survives in various manifestations. Its signal intent is to smooth away all hints of individualism or distinctiveness, which is why it so perfectly embodies the Dumbed-Down Decade. When Pete Townshend shoved the neck of his Gibson through the tweeter of a Marshall amp, he was making a statement. (Stupid, yes, but a statement.) When Kurt Cobain of Nirvana performed with hair he hadn't washed since the Gulf War, he was . . . well, performing with dirty hair. It wasn't even an anti-statement. It signified merely a lack—of pretense, or effort, or ambition. In one sense, this is old news. The upper classes always have enjoyed dressing down. In the eighties, when the wife of a Citicorp exec wore her jeans and T-shirt to an art gallery opening, she made sure to include the $2,300 Chanel handbag as a winking reference to her station. But now the class distinctions have vanished altogether. The dressing down reflects a genuine lack of taste. True to the trickle-down life cycle of trends, it is only a matter of time before grunge knockoffs are hanging from the racks at Kmart, which is, after all, where they came from in the first place.

Beyond the power chords of grunge, the music of the nineties has been influenced more decisively by the drum-machine ticky-tack of rap. From Elvis on, popular music has slowly been divesting itself of two of its components, melody and

harmony, emphasizing the third, rhythm. Rap relies on
rhythm alone and is thus perfectly democratic; relatively few
people can really carry a tune, and even fewer can harmo-
nize. Everyone can tap his toes.

As a social enterprise, the dumbing down of the nineties
entails more than an exaltation of the simple-minded and a
downgrading of the smart, and the blurring of the two as a
consequence. It also involves a reaction against achievement
itself, and particularly against the striving and ambition that
enable some people to pull away from the pack—to commit
the sin of inequality. The *New York Times* not long ago noted
efforts by educators to drain that fever swamp of inequality,
the school gym class. "Gym teachers," reported the *Times*,
"have thrown out their whistles and stop watches, telling students that it's all right to run at their own pace." Basketball
hoops are now adjustable, so that everyone can score. Those
of us who endured Coach Blutowski's gym class a generation ago will be shocked to discover that anyone could make
phys. ed. even stupider.

Assuming that any athletes emerge from the reformed gym
classes, they will feel at home in major-league baseball, as it
is being refined by the new spirit. The owners want another
round of playoffs—not merely for teams that finished first in
their divisions, but for second-place teams as well. The ethic
of the nineties makes good on the promise of Publishers
Clearing House: Everyone is a winner. Except, of course, for
those who are winning already.

You'd expect a zeitgeist so comprehensive to affect Washington's primary sport, public policy. And it has. The Clinton
administration may be ideologically fuzzy, but many of its
policy initiatives bear the decade's stamp. Most obvious was
the administration's fondest dream, the remaking of the
nation's health care system. By extending coverage to everyone and controlling cost by fiat, the administration would,

by the laws of economics, have curtailed the quality of care among those who now have the most access to it. This may be good public policy, but it is unmistakably rooted in a passion for leveling differences.

The administration's economic plan reflected the same passion. President Clinton's first budget, in its revival of progressive taxation, was frankly redistributionist. "We have to make sure," said Secretary of Commerce Ron Brown, "that the people who made out like bandits in the 1980s bear most of the burden." Not every rich guy is a bandit, of course, as Ron Brown, who was a millionaire several times over, would have admitted on sober reflection. But the rich made the mistake of pulling too far ahead. In the nineties they will be brought back to the herd.

Rich people were lionized in the 1980s; it's one of the clichés that defines the decade. The seminal business books of the time were *In Search of Excellence* and *Wealth and Poverty*, which exalted entrepreneurs as a special class of American, distinguished by their extraordinary drive, tenacity, and cleverness. (The author of *Wealth and Poverty*, George Gilder, was a disciple of Ayn Rand, who was in turn a bastardizer of Friedrich Nietzsche, inventor of the superman.) The men and women who created the nation's wealth *deserved* to be wealthy. Their success, according to the conventional wisdom, was earned. The levelers of the nineties recoil. Progressive tax rates proceed from the premise that the more money you make, the less you're entitled to it. Because achievement in commerce brings unequal rewards, the rewards should be diminished; it is equality's mandate. Recent business books reinforce the idea. The nineties version of *In Search of Excellence* is *Den of Thieves*, a recounting of the sins of Michael Milken, Ivan Boesky, and other gargoyles of the eighties. Without exception, businessmen are portrayed as rapacious and petty in the book's retelling. The accumulation of wealth itself begins to appear unsavory.

* * *

"Many that are first shall be last, and the last shall be first."
Defenders of the nineties can claim biblical support for their
mission. And certainly most of the leveling trends that char-
acterize the Dumbed-Down Decade were in train before the
nineties arrived, just as sixties communes had their roots in
Brook Farm. But is there, even theoretically, an end to the
equalizing? A point below which we cannot be dumbed down?
A lowest common denominator than which there is no denominator lower?

Only time, as the editorial writers like to say, will tell. The
forces in opposition to the nineties are even now coalescing.
They require, among much else, a charismatic figure to rally
'round. I offer a candidate for their consideration.

Ms. Adele Jones, of Millsboro, Delaware, was an algebra
teacher at Sussex Central High School. She was a tough
teacher, holding her students to a high standard. If they fell
below the standard, she failed them—as many as 42 percent
one year. By failing her students—those who, say her defenders, neglected to come to class, or who were unable to com-
pute percentages or perform simple addition—Jones fell out
of step with the times. The school board fired her.

While she appeals their decision, you can find her waiting
tables at a restaurant in sleepy Millsboro, a martyr to the
Dumbed-Down Decade.